The Passionate Edge

The Passionate Edge

LIVING A FULL LIFE IN AN EMPTY WORLD

Gloria Kempton

BROADMAN
& HOLMAN
PUBLISHERS

Nashville, Tennessee

© 1995 by Gloria Kempton
All rights reserved
Printed in the United States of America

Published by:
Broadman & Holman Publishers
Nashville, Tennessee

Design:
Steven Boyd

4261-53
0-8054-6153-1

Dewey Decimal Classification: 248.4
Subject Heading: Christian Life
Library of Congress Card Catalog Number: 95-12123

Unless otherwise noted, Scripture quotations are from the Holy Bible,
New International Version, copyright © 1973, 1978, 1984 by
International Bible Society.

Library of Congress Cataloging-in-Publication Data
Kempton, Gloria, 1951–
    The passionate edge : living a full life in an empty world / Gloria
Kempton
        p.   cm.
    ISBN 0-8054-6153-1
    1. Christian life. 2. Kempton, Gloria, 1951– . I. Title.
    BV4501.2.K4284   1995
    248.4—dc20
95-12123
CIP

99 98 97 96 95 5 4 3 2 1

▼

Dedicated to Ruby MacDonald and Lauraine Snelling,
my mentors in passion.

▼

Contents

▼

▼

ACKNOWLEDGMENTS

I wish to thank my editor, Vicki Crumpton, for believing in the manuscript and pushing me to be honest, positive, and kind in communicating my views on this subject that means so much to me—passion.

And then there's Kathy Boice, Brenda Wilbee, Michelle Cresse, Heather Harpham, and Traci Mullins—my sidekicks on the passionate journey. Without you, life would be Dullsville.

Lastly, I wish my mom were still around. I'd like to thank her for putting up with this bouncing-off-of-every-wall daughter of hers whose passion she did not always understand but whose passion she allowed—and encouraged.

———

▼

INTRODUCTION

Life is either a daring adventure or nothing."[1]

Profound words. I wish I'd spoken them. They were actually spoken many years ago by a blind and deaf mute named Helen Keller.

With all of her challenges, Helen Keller found life a daring adventure? So who am I to complain? But complain is exactly what I've done plenty of. Until a few years ago I would have described life as anything but a "daring adventure." Instead, I described it as a "pit of despair," one despairing day after another.

I remember the moment I realized that my present job was a losing endeavor. I spent my commuting time to and from work, crying. That should have told me something was wrong.

One day as a friend and I drove home, I whined once more about my job. As I climbed out of the car, I said, "I'd rather work at ————." (I named a well-known fast-food restaurant. I won't name it here because they actually have pretty good food.)

The minute I spoke the words I knew they were only too true. You know how you say some things and then laugh because you know you've exaggerated the issue? Well, this wasn't like that. I really meant what I said.

Now I don't believe that because we are unhappy somewhere, whether it's a job, marriage, or church, we're supposed to leave and go work at a fast-food restaurant or anywhere else. However, when the life is gone, it's time to take a look and find out exactly what God's up to.

The truth was, after a number of years and too many negative experiences, my heart for a once fulfilling job was gone, and I was now dead to it. That's the "nothing" that Helen Keller talks about.

In an emotional sense, I've gone through blindness, deafness, and muteness myself and would have to acknowledge Keller's statement as absolute truth. I made my decision long ago—if life can't be a daring adventure, I don't want it. And so, in partnership with God, "we" are now living a daring adventure.

Helen Keller understood "nothing"; otherwise, she couldn't have said what she did about life. For her, the only way to survive was to wake up to life—to conquer the nothing and discover the adventure.

I define this "life," this waking up, this adventure, with one word—*passion*. My daring adventure is the passion-filled life Jesus offers in John 10:10: "I have come that they may have life, and have it to the full."

Whether we ever consciously recognize it or not, we all arrive at that moment of decision where we must choose the kind of life we will live—one of nothing or one of passion. We are confronted with this decision many times, but if we choose nothing once, it becomes easy to choose it again. It is only as we choose passion—again and again and again—that life can truly become a daring adventure.

In John 10:10, the same Scripture that defines the full life for us, Jesus also tells us, "The thief comes only to steal and kill and destroy." Stripped of life, we're left with what?

Nothing. Sadly, this is where many of us live. We *let* the thief steal our passion. It's easier that way. We passively let life happen to us instead of confronting it, embracing it, and colliding with it. We refuse to take responsibility—we call ourselves victims and blame our passionless lives on others or circumstances. The thief succeeds in putting another of God's servants out of commission. Our cities and suburbs are graveyards full of live corpses. The thief laughs at his successful deception.

I know. I was one of those live corpses once. I died a complete death. And then . . .

In one sense we must all die before we can live. It's the great paradox of the gospel. When our death is orchestrated by God, even though it's painful, it works out quite well. Unfortunately, my death wasn't orchestrated by God (I gave up and did it to myself), and toward the end, I felt the Holy One and the Evil One, the thief, in a battle for my soul.

We must understand the battles in the supernatural that suspend us between life and death. All along the way we make choices that take the battle in one direction or another. We may not consciously recognize that we're making choices, but we are; if we're not consciously directing the battle, we're doing so unconsciously. My most important goal in this book is to wake you up and make you aware of the battle and your choices so that you might not choose nothing, but that you might choose the daring adventure—the passion-filled life.

O N E

▼

TACTICS OF THE THIEF

What do Michaelangelo, Whitney Houston, and Mother Teresa have in common?

Time's up. How about Martin Luther King Jr., Billy Graham, and Oprah Winfrey?

Quite a diverse group. What do they have in common? The answer can be summed up in one word—*passion*. Each one of these individuals lived or lives with tremendous passion for a chosen and very specific calling.

Well, then, what about Tonya Harding, Dr. Jack Kevorkian, and Michael Jackson? They, too, are people of passion. What about Adolph Hitler, David Koresh, and Ted Bundy? If what they share can also be called passion, it makes us wonder if this compelling drive is something we should pursue.

If passion can turn a person into a monster, we could certainly be justified if we fear that this could happen to us. On the other hand, if passion makes great painters, singers, and orators, we have to take a serious look at it and ask ourselves if this is something that God wants for us?

There are any number of sax players performing in clubs, restaurants, and concerts all over the world.

And then there's Kenny G.

Christian writers have been putting their pens to paper for centuries. Our Christian bookstores are bulging.

And then there's C. S. Lewis.

The vocalists who have blessed our lives with their voices are too numerous to count.

And then there's Barbra Streisand.

Their passion took them to the top. No, you don't have to become rich or famous. But your passion can make you great in life—in the ways that count. Only you know what God has whispered deep down in your soul when you've asked Him, "What do you want to do with my life?"

Is Your Passion Alive?

The passion-filled life is one full of physical, intellectual, social, emotional, and spiritual movement.

In this book, I'd like to challenge you to examine the movement, stirrings, and growth or lack thereof in your life. For it's only in conducting such an examination that you can make a conscious decision whether or not you want to pursue life on the passionate edge.

The thief's job, according to John 10:10, is to "steal and kill and destroy." This is what he works hard at all day, every day. If he can't kill our passion, he'll work to destroy it by scaring us (after all, we might go *over* the edge) or by wearing us down (living passionately takes a lot of energy). If he can't destroy it, he'll steal it by making us too spiritual to pursue such a "carnal" goal as passion.

I call it the passionate edge. Helen Keller called it a daring adventure. Jesus Christ calls it the abundant life.

Let's try not to get sidetracked with semantics. The most important thing to know is that the abundant and passionate life is God's plan for us. Since the One who promised us a passionate life was Jesus Christ, if you decide to take the challenge, you have to believe there's a way to walk along the edge without falling off. At least that's the goal.

Sure, I've fallen off a few times. I'm glad God's hands are big enough to catch me and that He's the Great Redeemer of my falling-off times. If it were left to me to pick up the pieces each time, that's all I'd be doing. I'd have no time or energy to walk along the edge.

Before we can explore how to approach the passionate edge and learn to maneuver without falling off, we must understand a bit about numbness, death, or whatever you want to call what the "thief" does to keep us far from the edge and absolutely useless to the kingdom of God and His redemptive plan.

As I said earlier, the areas of passion include our physical, intellectual, social, emotional, and spiritual lives. The thief has a strategy for targeting these five areas that we must be aware of before we can move forward in our pursuit of the passionate life.

Saggy Muscles

My friend Lynne and I were driving home from another friend's house one day when I noticed the first snowflakes of winter drop lightly onto my windshield. I felt a stirring. Passion? Yes, I feel passionate about snow. I love it. However, I also felt terror on this particular day. I never, repeat, never, drive in the snow. I'm from the West Coast, not the Midwest. I don't drive in snow. Not ever.

Another thing I'm terrified of is looking like a wimp in front of other people. I kept driving, mentally calculating the miles between where we were and home. At least forty miles were left.

"Oh, look, it's snowing," I said lightly, trying to keep the tremor out of my voice. The flakes (more than one had fallen by this point) were bigger now.

"Isn't it pretty?" Lynne remarked.

"Beautiful," I said, as I turned on my wipers. They didn't work very well, and I could only see through a small corner of my windshield.

I knew I was going to die. Probably any minute. A semi wouldn't be able to stop and would wipe us off the road. I started planning my funeral, not that I'd get to tell anyone how I wanted it to go. However, I always like to picture who will be there.

I watched the snow grow deeper on the side of the freeway. If it were going to happen, I wished it would hurry up. I've always been the kind of person who jumps into the icy water, not one who agonizingly inches her way in. If I were going to die anyway, I wanted to get it over with.

I have a van that slides on a piece of paper. I dropped Lynne off after driving thirty-eight tension-filled miles and crept the rest of the way home.

Three blocks from my driveway, the highway starts a gradual descent. I applied the brakes ever so lightly. The van swung its rear end around and slid into the other lane, heading for the line of oncoming cars. I waited for the impact and certain oblivion—my death. I shut my eyes. I'm such a wimp. If Lynne could only see me now.

The van stopped. No crash. I opened my eyes. We (my van and I) were about an inch from the front end of a small parked car. Drivers on the highway maneuvered their way around us.

Ever so delicately, I backed my van up, parked behind the little car, and walked the three blocks home, enjoying every minute of my brisk walk in the snow.

A very recent and poignant reminder of my level of passion for anything—physical activity or element of nature—that might threaten my physical life. My passion in this area can better be described as—paralyzing fear.

OK, I know what you're thinking. Let's set the record straight. You don't have to have achieved perfection in every area in order to write a book about it.

I'm working on it—not achieving perfection, but confronting my physical fears. A couple of years ago a friend consistently invited me along whenever she went river-rafting, bungee jumping, or snowmobiling. I consistently made up excuses as to why I couldn't accompany her on her various excursions. Eventually she quit asking. I missed many opportunities to grow.

However, I have a seventy-one-year-old friend who regularly rides the waves in a raft, treks across the African countryside on safari, and makes mad passionate love to her husband in exotic lands. She's my mentor and a passion-lover if I ever saw one. Pursuing physical passion is high on her to-do list, and she is one of the most alive people I know.

Physical passion encompasses many things; our energy level and/or our endurance, our willingness to try new sports or physical activities, our courage in facing death, and our ability to express our sexuality, to name a few. Since I'm committed to honesty in this book, I have to admit that over the last few years the last one is the one in which I've grown the most.

Oh, I can guess what you're thinking again. *She's a single woman, how can she be growing in her ability to express her sexuality?* I don't quite know how to say this, but if you're married and have ever wondered about your single friends, yes, we singles can be very much sexually alive. I didn't say sexually active. Sexually alive. (I hate being misunderstood. I wrote an article for a Christian magazine once on how to have the sex talk with your kids. They received many hot letters because I said we should tell our kids that sex should be saved for a "special relationship." I neglected to say that special relationship should be marriage. Wrong choice of words. But I didn't do it deliberately.)

So, to make this really clear, when I say I'm growing in my ability to express my sexuality, I'm not talking about the physical act of sex, but the celebration of my femininity.

Still, as singles, unless God has called us and given us the gift of celibacy (another book—not this one), I think it's a shame to let our sexual and sensual passion die. You never know when you might need it.

In marriage, it's absolutely tragic when sexual passion dies. Yet, in more marriages than we'd like to think, passion is gone. It's not something we go around talking about ("Hi, Denise, how's yours and Jim's sexual passion these days?"), so who knows what the statistics are, but we can take a pretty good guess. All we have to do is listen to how our friends talk about their spouses. Even more revealing is what they don't say about their spouses.

Whew—in a book on passion, I just knew we'd have to talk about sex. I'm glad to get it over with in the first chapter.

The point is, the thief wants to destroy our physical passion. That's one reason we're so often too tired to work out, too scared to parachute, and, for those of us who are married, uninterested in sex.

Later, we'll see how we can conquer our fears and weariness and approach the passionate edge, but right now we need to understand what the hindrances are and why we give into them.

Stirring Our Brain Waves

I have heard "knowledge puffs up" (1 Cor. 8:1) used many times by those who have no interest in pursuing intellectual growth. I always wonder what God thinks when we use Scripture as an excuse for not pursuing those things we're too lazy or afraid to deal with. This is another way the thief steals our passion—through Scripture itself. Or, I should say the misuse of Scripture.

Knowledge can indeed puff up. We all know power-hungry people who attain great leadership positions because they're so smart, or think they are. But just because someone misuses knowledge, that doesn't mean knowledge is something to scorn. David Koresh used Scripture to build a cult following. That doesn't mean we now scorn the Bible.

Scripture also holds up Solomon as an example of one of the wisest and most knowledgeable men who ever lived. The Bible says, "When the queen of Sheba heard of Solomon's fame, she came to Jerusalem to test him with hard questions. . . . Solomon answered all her questions; nothing was too hard for him to explain to her" (2 Chron. 9:1–2). To me, this says that God values intellectual passion, the desire to learn and know.

The thief knows that if he can destroy our intellectual passion, he can keep us in a childish, naive, super-spiritual place that approaches life so simplistically the power to influence others is greatly diminished. While there's a place for approaching the gospel in a simple and childlike way, without true intellectual passion, we demand answers where there are none, answer questions no one is asking, and approach every issue from a black or white viewpoint.

Jesus told His followers, that's you and me, to "love the Lord your God with all your . . . mind" (Matt. 22:37). Learning, asking questions, reading, listening, interacting with all kinds of folks—we must grow in our minds if we are to grow in our capacity to love God.

To live fully alive in the intellectual arena is to: (Some of the following suggestions are considered controversial; they're marked with asterisks.)

▼ read books, magazines, and newspapers that challenge our thinking;*

▼ take college classes that challenge our thinking;*

▼ cultivate friendships with the kind of people who challenge our thinking;*

▼ watch talk shows and go to movies that challenge our thinking; and*

▼ dare to ask questions that challenge our thinking.*

Every so often I become mentally restless, irritable, and hungry, but not for food. My passion for intellectual stimulation needs attention.

11

▼

My longing for intellectual stimulation recently drove me to attend a seminar led by author Scott Peck. It was sponsored by a denominational church that I've often heard referred to as a cult.

This was my first challenge—to put aside my biases about this particular church and open my mind to both God and Peck. I went, eager to receive and grow.

The audience's questions were not ones I would have asked and Peck's "answers," if they could be called that, were not the ones I would have expected.

Peck kept answering, "I don't know," to more questions than most of us felt comfortable with. Strangely enough, with each "I don't know," I became more comfortable. Then he taught us to say those three words.

"Say it after me," he instructed. "I . . . don't . . . know."

"I . . . don't . . . know," we repeated. We repeated it again and again.

The more I spoke the words, the more I felt the freedom to speak the words. For the next few weeks, I kept hoping someone would ask me a question that I didn't have an answer to so I could say, "I don't know."

Peck challenged my intellect. I didn't have to have all the answers, for myself or anyone else. God has them.

My intellectual passion is now fueled by the freedom to ask the kind of questions that don't have answers. As I'm growing, my questions are moving from "Why?" to "How?" and "What?" Less often I ask *why* homelessness, pain, suffering, AIDS, madness. More often I ask *how* can I move redemptively? *What* can I do?

This is staying on the passionate edge. The reason the thief wants to steal our intellectual passion is so that he can keep us inactive and ineffective, distracting us from the real issues. If he can keep us contemptuous of intellectual passion, he can keep us from growing. He is aware of the potential of the mind that is truly committed to Christ's redemptive work. He knows how much more powerful we will become if we continue to learn and grow in our minds.

What's Your Name?

I call it social passion. It's the longing to know and be known. It's the need for community. Author and scholar Paula Gunn Allen once said, "Snowflakes, leaves, humans, plants, raindrops, stars, molecules, microscopic entities all come in communities. The singular cannot in reality exist."[1]

God intends for us to live in community. Those who don't feel the need for others, who experience little or no social passion, have probably been burned somewhere along the way—maybe once, maybe many times.

The thief works hard to keep us away from each other, create distance between us, and make us mad at each other.

The most significant relationship of my life started with three little words: "What's your name?" I asked the question, never imagining the relational experience that would occur as a result. However, I was open to it as was the other person.

Of course, as we all know, to the degree that we love in our relationships, we also hurt. When I started to experience pain in relating to this individual, I immediately closed up. As a matter of fact, we joked about my "turtle shell." When I was hurt, no matter how hard anyone pounded, I would not come out until I was good and ready.

Through a series of choices and healings, I learned that I can only pursue the passionate edge outside of my shell. I hardly ever retreat anymore. I'm too afraid I might miss something.

We can choose with whom we spend time. One way the thief destroys our social passion is to bring one too many people into our lives who drain us with their problems and negativity. Now, granted, I have my negative, complaining days. On those days I try to stay away from people so I'm not the one responsible for draining someone's social passion.

▼

Don't we all know individuals who seem to consider it their mission in life to make the rest of us miserable? Just so you know, our social passion is drained whenever we spend too much time with those who:

▼ thwart our goals;

▼ consistently criticize us or those we love;

▼ have a value system that opposes ours;

▼ approach life from a negative viewpoint;

▼ and have a personal and selfish agenda such as gaining control of, manipulating, and/or using us.

We cannot totally avoid these people. What if the person who drains us is a husband, child, or coworker? What if we have little control, if circumstances are such that we're constantly thrown together with those who sap our energy? The only thing we can do is determine to spend a limited amount of time with them, no more than we have to.

If their influence is affecting me negatively and nothing seems to be getting better, I will eventually find a way to remove myself from their presence—sometimes permanently. My passion (not to mention my sanity) is too precious.

Like you, I'm invited to showers, receptions, in-home parties, and other social gatherings organized for the purpose of selling, celebrating, or grieving. I hate them. Yet, I know that if I don't ever take the opportunity to ask the question, "What's your name?" I'll soon be living my life quite alone.

I met someone at a barbecue once who over the years has become a good friend. I didn't want to go. I hated being there. The conversation was superficial. Now I'm glad I went and did the small talk routine. I can't imagine my life without Jan.

Some of us have too much social passion. We attend every church activity and every event at our kids' school and look for every excuse to golf or go to a movie with a friend. What is driving this compulsion? It could be the need to escape some kind of internal pain.

Social passion could be called people passion. God calls us to love one another. Jesus said, "All men will know that you are my disciples, if you love one another" (John 13:35).

Can you imagine why the thief might want to keep us apart? Kill our social passion? Make us mad at each other?

Yes, sometimes we really bug each other, annoy each other, and hurt each other. And without God's kind of connecting passion, we truly can destroy each other.

We can only count on God extending His love, mercy, and grace to each of us so that we might be empowered to keep forgiving and extending ourselves to each other. It's up to us to keep our passion alive.

The Guts of It

Michaelangelo, the passionate painter I mentioned at the beginning of this chapter, spoke these words at his time of death. "Life has been good. God did not create me to abandon me. I have loved marble, yes, and paint too. I have loved architecture, and poetry too. I have loved my family and my friends. I have loved God, the forms of the earth and the heavens, and people, too. I have loved life to the full."

How many of us can say that about our lives—that we "loved life to the full"?

He was even able to say, "and now I love death as its natural termination."[2]

He even loved and embraced his own death. For Michelangelo, life was definitely a daring adventure.

I decided a few years ago that I was going to engage my guts in this thing called life. I made this decision when I was in the deepest, darkest hole of my entire life. The thief had not only stolen my emotional passion; he had destroyed it, killed it.

My life now in the present is a tribute to the redemptive power of God, and a confirmation that we can recover the gift of passion that God gives to each of His children at birth.

I was a passionate and creative child. I would ask, "Mom, can I have some of your paper?"

My mom must have given me reams of paper during my childhood. I cut, pasted it together, and colored it to make towns. I drew my own paper dolls and made clothes. I played in the street with my friends every night, playing kick-the-can, hide-and-seek, and prison ball. I collected caterpillars and bumblebees. I played with an imaginary friend, Francis. I pretended I was a movie star, a Beatles, and a nun.

I remember myself as a teenager, asking, "Mom, can I have some of your paper?"

I wrote stories, long fictional tales about me and my friends. I cruised around in my red 1965 Mustang with my friends, picking up boys and having other adventures. I was president of one of the girls clubs in our school, and I served as student body historian. I was in the Pep Club. I had lots of girlfriends and boyfriends. I loved people and every day was a party.

I remember myself as a young bride. No time to create things out of paper anymore. Still excited, my creativity and my energy went into my new husband and having five babies. This was my life now, and I would live it well.

I'm not sure when it all began sucking more energy out of me than I had to give. I don't know whether it was the stress of my abusive marriage, the demands of five children, or the image I held at that time of a God who would settle for no less than perfection from this sinner.

All I know is I started to lose it. It was a gradual process. I didn't lose it all at once. I just began to lose momentum a little bit at a time.

It started with my kids. They were everywhere all of the time.

"Mom, I need . . ."

"Mom, I want . . ."

"Mom, give me . . ."

Something. Everything. Now. How could I give them everything they wanted? How could I be everything they needed? Ever?

Next, I knew my marriage was not going to work. I'd tried everything I knew how to try. It was only getting worse, and I was tired.

Finally, I was pretty sure God was upset with me. Since I thought He required perfection and I couldn't be perfect, I knew I was a disappointment to Him. I couldn't measure up and knew I never would be able to. The raw truth was I was tired of trying.

Now what? Where do you go? What do you do when you are totally exhausted, discouraged, and completely unaware that anything could ever be any different? Or better? Or that full and passionate aliveness is available?

It was a long road back, but I understand now that we can't truly appreciate something until we've lost it.

The following chapters are full of ways to recover lost passion and to maintain our walk on the passionate edge once we've found it.

One thing I'm learning about emotional passion is that it fuels all of the other passions. Without that deep feeling of excitement and enthusiasm in our gut, we can't push ourselves in any direction. Our motor is broken and rubber bands just don't fix it.

Life without love (emotional passion) is not life at all. Once we've loved and been loved deeply, by God and at least one significant other, there's no turning back to embrace death. Maybe I'm naive, but it's beyond my comprehension that the thief could ever touch my emotional passion now. I'm committed to it.

Igniting the Spirit

No one was ever more excited as a new Christian than I was. I bought every Christian book and record as soon as it was released. I went to church three and four times a week. I devoured chapters of the Bible every day. My spiritual passion was alive and well.

▼

How can something so alive die such a complete death? The thief destroyed every bit of my zeal for God and the spiritual life. Have you ever been there? Maybe you just feel yourself slipping, and it panics you a bit? Maybe you've felt it for a long time, but have never acknowledged it to anyone for fear of his or her reaction. Maybe you haven't even acknowledged it to yourself.

Maybe you know someone who's far from the passionate edge in his or her spiritual life and it concerns you. However, when you try to talk to this person, you hit a wall.

Spiritual Abuse

A few years ago a friend of mine dealt with some spiritual abuse in her life and began struggling in her relationships. She stopped talking the talk ("God told me . . . ") because she wasn't sure what God's voice sounded like anymore. She no longer walked the walk (she missed church quite often, read her Bible infrequently, and prayed only when she could) because she wasn't sure what the walk looked like anymore.

Her friends were concerned, understandably so. Unfortunately, their concern came through as judgment: "What do you mean you're not going to church as often?" "So what's the Lord been saying to you in the Word lately?"

My friend was at a loss. "I don't know what to tell them," she would mourn. "I guess the best thing to do is not to talk about it at all."

Too many people don't understand spiritual abuse, and it takes so much out of the victim to explain it.

Fortunately my friend is now recovering her spiritual passion. She's found a church that doesn't keep track of her attendance, but whose members simply greet her warmly when she shows up. She's making new friends who are not questioning and challenging her lack of spiritual progress, but encouraging and cheering when she takes a baby step—reads even one Bible verse or asks prayer for a seemingly insignificant area of her life. The thief has not ultimately destroyed my friend's spiritual

▼

passion. I'm convinced she'll come back stronger than ever before in her pursuit of the spiritual journey.

Spiritual Overload

Of course, spiritual abuse is not the only way the thief steals our spiritual passion. He burns us out. We work so hard on spiritual endeavors that we eventually overload.

We get to the place where there isn't anything to be excited about anymore. I remember twenty years ago at the height of the Jesus movement and the charismatic movement, everyone was preaching on street corners, shouting in churches, and rapidly turning Bible pages. People held rallies, attended crusades, and spoke in tongues.

No wonder we now have a recovery movement! We need one after all that frenetic activity.

Our spiritual passion has suffered a tremendous blow in how we view our leaders. Highly regarded evangelists like Jim Bakker and Jimmy Swaggart had highly publicized falls. A lot of spiritually-minded people looked up to these men over the years. Even if you're not a fan of this wing of Christianity, live long enough and you'll see someone—a pastor, a youth leader, a spiritual hero—fall.

So we've become cynical and disillusioned. We're a hurting people, and I'm not one for covering up the truth. The worst thing we can do is to try to hide our blemishes from the world, keep our image intact, and keep our "testimony" pure. This particular effort is what has earned us the reputation of "hypocrites." We know how Jesus felt about the hypocrites in His day—the Pharisees and Sadducees.

Moving Toward the Edge

If covering up and pretense isn't the answer, what is? I believe the answer lies in the recovery of our passion. Passionate people never have to pretend. They experience genuine physical aliveness, intellectual stimulation, social awareness, emotional wholeness, and spiritual progress every single day.

Sound like the impossible dream? Not at all. If you've lived most of your life cautiously approaching the edge, peering over, running back to safety, cautiously feeling your way back again, ad nauseum, you can change.

You can be one of those who dives to the edge, runs along it, does handstands and cartwheels, and hangs one leg over—loving every minute of it.

It's quite possible.

——

T W O

▼

HIDING PLACES

W e'll find out who's the toughest when I beat Renae up tomorrow," Amber mumbled as she rinsed the dishes in the sink, her daily chore at our house.

Had I heard her right? Had I just heard my sweet little twelve-year-old say she was going to beat up someone the next day?

"You'll win, too," my fourteen-year-old, Merilee, commented. "Renae's a wimp."

"What are you talking about?" I asked.

"Oh nothing," Amber said.

"Amber's going to beat up Renae tomorrow after school," Merilee explained quite casually. "It's all planned."

Amber looked a little sheepish. "She called me a name today and I opened my umbrella in her face. So we're going to fight. It's been coming for a long time."

"I can't believe it. No way. Have you prayed about this?" I didn't know how I was supposed to react to this news.

"Yeah. I asked God to forgive me for what I know I have to do," said Amber.

Later, I heard my son out in the front room coaching his sister in various moves, how to show she wasn't afraid, and how to be aggressive. They were laughing, and for some reason, maybe because Amber didn't really seem that mad at Renae who was at one time a close friend, I didn't think the fight would happen. I forgot about it.

It did happen and everyone got suspended from school, including Merilee who was in the front of the crowd egging the fight on. She had always loved drama and action.

When I was in school it seldom occurred to us to resolve our problems with one another by fighting. Oh, I remember once in fourth grade I planned to fight another girl after school, but it was nothing. We danced around each other for a few minutes and ended up laughing and renewing our friendship. Maybe this is why I didn't take Amber's fight seriously.

Now I'm concerned. This is just a tiny example of how things have changed since I was in school. Everywhere we turn people are resorting to violence and abuse to resolve conflicts. I'll leave researching the reasons behind our anti-social and depraved behavior to other authors. What's important for us to realize as we think about living on the passionate edge is how dealing with daily violence and abuse can rob us of our focus to act passionately and redemptively in our world.

In Seattle, one of the major news stations is placing special emphasis on a program called "Stop the Violence." Each night they approach this social malady from a different angle and offer solutions that we, as individuals, can apply to our daily lives and in our personal worlds. Not only are we becoming more aware of the problem, but we are discovering creative solutions. Have you ever noticed that people wait until violence or abuse touches them personally before they do anything? Maybe this is normal. Maybe an issue has to touch us before it touches us deeply, if you know what I mean. Our anger over a violent act committed against us or our loved ones often motivates us to take action of some kind.

Unfortunately, the prevailing emotion that often surfaces in us when faced with a violent society is not anger but fear. We're afraid that:

▼ we or our loved ones might get hurt,

▼ the "bad" people might take over,

▼ we might suffer loss of property and/or security,

▼ God won't do anything to protect us,

▼ or, we might die.

We fear other minor things, but those are probably the big ones.

The tragic thing is that we allow fear to prevail, and it paralyzes us and crowds out our passion. Why? Because the moment we choose to let fear drive us in life, we make another automatic choice—to spend our energy protecting ourselves from whatever it is we're afraid of.

Facing the Fear Factor

I can't remember the exact day that fear began driving my life, goals, and ambitions and crowding out my passion. It was a gradual process. All I know is that one day I started experiencing terrifying panic attacks, and it wasn't long after that I became almost agoraphobic. I was in my twenties, too young to die this kind of horrible internal death. But die I did, totally and completely—passionless, without a spark of life.

I was afraid of a lot of things:

▼ people looking at me funny

▼ hell (newly divorced, I just knew I'd gotten on God's last nerve)

▼ crowds

▼ Christian men

▼ church

▼ the "world"

The list was endless. I didn't feel safe anywhere. Paranoid beyond belief, I searched frantically for anything and everything that might protect me from my fears. This is what I did all day every day. I used all of my energy trying to find ways to stay safe from the "scary stuff."

This might sound extreme, but think about your own fears. What are you afraid of? Are you afraid to openly disagree with a friend, afraid of conflict? Are you afraid your spouse finds you unattractive? Are you afraid of being alone at night? Are you afraid of homosexuals and abortionists? Once you've acknowledged your fears, think about how much of your time and energy are spent protecting yourself.

I remember the day I walked into Disneyland for the first time since I was ten years old. I was thirty-five. I looked around and panicked. I couldn't go on any of the rides, at least not the important ones like The Matterhorn or Space Mountain. I was too scared. What if . . . what if . . . what if what? What was I scared of? Looking back, I think I was afraid of fear itself. Fear had violated me in violent ways, and I never deliberately put myself in a position to be scared.

I'd wanted to come back to Disneyland for years. I loved walking into a fantasyland of cartoon characters, colorful parades, and adventuresome train and boat rides. Yet, part of Disneyland was the scary rides.

"Let's go!" my friend said and took off toward the long line at Space Mountain. "I love this one."

My other friend followed. Then and there I made a decision. I would go on every single ride in that place if it killed me, and I knew it might. Disneyland was so close to my heart; I had to overcome my fear. I didn't want to be afraid of such a magical wonderland.

I went on every single ride that day and many of them twice. I staggered off Space Mountain, my heart in my throat. I'd conquered my fear, and it felt great. I wanted to get right back on. The Matterhorn was one of my favorites; the thrill of speeding up that mountain and back down again stayed with me all day. A few years later when Splash Mountain was added, I swallowed my fear and climbed into the front car.

Disneyland is one of my passions. I go there at least once a year and sometimes twice, whenever I need time away from the daily grind and when I need to passionately abandon myself and embrace—my fears.

Releasing our fears is not usually as easy as going to Disneyland and making a decision to go on all the rides. Since fear creeps up on us, we are often unconscious of the way we choose to deal with it. We all do deal with it. Over and over in Scripture, Jesus said, "Do not fear" because He knew we would.

Fear and its effects are complicated issues in our lives, but I have observed that, as Christians, we choose to deal with fear in three common ways; we become "rules addicts" or "preachers" or enter into "the nice little Christian" syndrome.

The Rules Addict

As a new Christian (and as an "old" one, but that's irrelevant), I was sometimes tempted to smoke. When I got mad at my new husband, I would go out and buy a pack of cigarettes, lock myself in the bathroom, and puff away. "The Bible says, 'Your body is a temple of the Holy Spirit.' No smoking," he would call through the door. (The underlying message was that "God will get you if you smoke.") No smoking—that was the rule. It was a simple matter to memorize this rule.

As a new Christian, the first time I swore at my husband, he cuffed me a good one. "You can't swear," he told me. "But now you must rid yourselves of all such things as . . . filthy language from your lips." I learned the biblical rule that day—no swearing.

I learned the rules about drinking, sexual sins, gossiping (that was a hard one to follow), love of money, friendship with "the world," dancing, ad infinitum. The underlying rule was "Don't do anything—or God will get you."

My goal became to learn and memorize as many rules as I could to stay ahead of God before He "got" me.

It wore me out. Even if you come up with a million rules, who can keep them? That's why God sent Jesus. It took me a long time to figure this out and by the time I did, I was exhausted.

Whether consciously or unconsciously, we jump onto this treadmill in our everyday lives. A fear approaches, and we make up a rule. Then we run in circles as we work hard to keep the rule and make sure that others do, as well.

▼ *Fear:* "Jerry is talking way too much about that new assistant in his office. What if he has an affair?"
Rule: No friendships with anyone of the opposite sex.

▼ *Fear:* "Violence is becoming the order of the day."
Rule: Three strikes, you're out. Lock up everyone on his or her third offense. (My home state of Washington came up with this one, only now they're re-evaluating because the first candidate to be convicted under the new law is a petty thief.)

▼ Fear: "Hollywood is so 'worldly.'"
Rule: No movies.

If you're afraid, make up a rule. However, did God intend for us to use all of our spiritual energy, our gift of the passion-filled life trying to keep a million rules and then running around trying to enforce them?

The Preacher

When faced with violence and abuse, out of our fear, many of us become preachers. We put our passion and energy into talking. We talk about guns in school. We talk about domestic violence. We talk about child abuse. All of which are important issues. If I may digress for a moment, I wonder if we were to use our passion to fight child abuse alone, how many of society's problems would simply disappear.

Because we hear ourselves talking so much, it may begin to feel like we're doing something. The truth is we're staying far away from the passionate edge if all we're doing is talking. Fear makes most of us talk. The more afraid we are, the faster we talk. We quote Scripture verses loud and long. The louder and longer, the more confidence we have of their working.

A man in my area is campaigning long and loud against the homosexual community. He shows up on the news, pops up at local churches, gets measures on every ballot, and thinks he's doing God and the Christian community a big favor. He's driven by fear. Of what? Possibly his own unresolved sexual issues. He may be doing penance for past sexual sins of his own. He may be serving an angry god who he's working hard to appease.

Out of his misguided spiritual passion, his anger and hatred are doing incredible damage and overshadowing any good that God may bring out of this man's campaign. I'm thankful that God is a redeemer.

I'm left having to use some of my precious passion to forgive this angry man for what I see as a terrible misrepresentation of God and the Christian community.

The "Nice Little Christian" Syndrome

When fears surface, many people immediately think if they're just nice enough, the problems will go away (just for the record, I was never one of them). I knew someone who would begin to sing every time something scary happened. For some reason, this was terribly annoying.

One time the "singer," two other friends, and I experienced car trouble on the freeway. We were miles away from an exit and as we tried to figure out what to do, we all became slightly irritated with one another.

"I think two of us should walk for help."

"It's getting dark, and it's at least five miles to the nearest exit. Which two were you thinking of?"

"It's not five miles, and quit being a wimp. I suppose you want to stay here and pray someone comes along to rescue us?"

"Yeah, a psycho-killer, no doubt."

"God wouldn't send a psycho-killer."

"I don't know. Did you hear about that woman . . ."

That's when she started to sing. "This is the day, this is the day that the Lord has made, that the Lord has made. We will rejoice, we will rejoice . . . "

We stared at our friend, dumbfounded.

"No point in getting all upset." She smiled broadly. "This is the day, this is the day . . . "

To this day I still think she's lucky we didn't make her walk five miles for help all by herself.

I have known many of these types—those who believe if they express any other emotion than spiritual ecstasy, they are sinning. They use their passion and energy to repress their real feelings so they can keep smiling and smooth over the problem, whatever it is.

Genuine joy is a process. Because we're not Jesus Christ personified but human beings, I believe that when in trouble we can only express true joy when we've expressed our human emotions first—anger, fear, sorrow, whatever the situation surfaces in us.

The "nice little Christian" is sincere, believing that prayer, forgiveness, love, grace, evangelization, and other Christian principles are all we need to equip us to face this evil world. This person will continue to believe this until tragedy hits and none of these are enough to protect him or her from the suffering that follows. A child is molested, a *Christian* child. A home burns, a *Christian* home. A family is murdered, a *Christian* family.

I remember one bright spring day in 1980 when I began to question some beliefs of my own about suffering and the Christian. In the early morning hours of this particular day a man broke into a family's home and brutally stabbed each family member, a mom, dad and two children. In 1980, senseless murders weren't the commonplace act they are now, but what terrified me was that this was a Baptist family. These people were Christians and lovers of God.

Obviously, the rule "Thou shall not murder" (Exod. 20:13) hadn't saved this God-loving family. I guess somewhere inside I had hoped that the "nice little Christians" had the answer if I didn't. However, you can't just walk up to a murderer, tell him "Jesus loves you—repent," and heal the problem.

A community was shattered. A gripping fear invaded people's lives. For loved ones who weren't able to cope, life stopped on that day.

Significant to the Christian community, where was the passion needed to confront this tragedy? Instead of taking passionate action, everyone started asking questions to which they would never find answers: "Where was God?" "Where was our faith?" "It happened to them; couldn't it happen to me?"

They coped by praying more intensely, attending more Bible studies, and working harder to make sure they were forgiving the man who murdered that family. Don't get me wrong. Praying, studying, and forgiving are all essential to our faith. But they focus on the internal. Sometimes we need to emphasize the external, too. We need to take action to change the circumstances which contribute to evil.

Staying Too Safe

It really is scary out there, and getting scarier. We can't minimize that. Sometimes when I run to the store and back, I think, "Wow, I wasn't mugged, raped, or killed. I survived out there another day."

For those of you who live in small towns and are unaccustomed to daily crime, you may not have a clue as to what I'm talking about. Count your blessings. I live in what was once called "the most livable city" in the United States. No longer. We're catching up with Detroit and Los Angeles in the crime arena. Last month, one kid killed another for his jacket.

▼

It makes me sad, but I make daily decisions to confront my fears so that I can live passionately in the city I fell in love with ten years ago.

We only have two choices—live fearfully or live passionately. If we have never before consciously and deliberately acknowledged this choice, we've chosen fear.

We may think we're safe because we've moved to the suburbs, locked our doors and windows, and enrolled our children in private schools. The opposite is true. Fear is a prison of the worst kind, and it robs us of our passion for living.

Worst of all, we've missed the whole point of life on this planet. When we choose to use our God-given passion to stay safe, we deny Christ's power for the purpose to which He's called us. We are here to be God's redemptive agents, leading a dark world to the light.

Denying Christ's Power

Because God has called us to the passionate privilege of working alongside Him in His redemptive plan, we deny His power when we do any less. Running, living in fear, and obsessively trying to stay safe are definitely less than what He has planned for us.

Specifically, we deny Christ's power and waste our passion when we:

▼ enable and refuse to confront a spouse, child, or anyone in our home who is abusive toward others;

▼ live in paralyzing fear of anyone or anything; and

▼ make staying safe our goal.

Jesus fought a long, hard battle with the enemy of His soul (and ours) in the wilderness. He fought again in the Garden of Gethsemane sweating drops of blood as He battled. He fought on the cross as momentarily, even His Father abandoned Him. He did all this for us. His power is ours.

I faced a hard choice recently. My daughter burst into my bedroom one day proclaiming her love for Eric, a boy I only knew as the older brother of her best friend. "I love him!" she told me in a voice truly meant one day for the stage.

My heart sank. Eric was a known gang member. Every cop in the neighborhood knew Eric. They'd arrest him on sight for wearing his hat backward. What could I say? *No, you can't love him?*

I gulped, "You do?" I had to stall for time. "Didn't you tell me he was in a gang?" *That's it. Give her a chance to lie so that I don't have to deal with this, at least not today.*

"Yeah, but he's getting out," she said.

Sure, I thought.

"Well, uh, maybe we'd better go out to dinner so I can get to know him if he's, uh, someone who means a lot to you," I told her.

She hugged me and waltzed out of the room. I let out the breath I'd held the entire time I'd given her all that stuff about going out to dinner. All I really wanted to do was move away where there were only nice boys and girls.

A week later we went to dinner, and I began to understand why she'd fallen in love with Eric. He was polite. He opened the car door and waited for my daughter and me to go into the restaurant first. He was honest. "Ask me anything," he said as he smiled and buttered his bread. He knew he was on trial and answered every one of my questions without hesitation. He was kind. "You want to watch a video tonight with us?" he asked me, an old woman, after dinner was over.

However, it soon became apparent that Eric had an anger problem. "I'll throw rocks and knock out every window of your house!" he screamed at my daughter one time during a fight.

During another fight, when my daughter went to his house to visit his sister, he spotted her in his yard and called her every rotten name he could think of.

Being true to his word, he removed himself from the gang and stopped smoking pot. He knew these things weren't good

▼

for him and that I disapproved. He'd broken down in front of me and cried more than once.

"You can't threaten us like that," I confronted him after the rock throwing comment.

"I'm so sorry," he cried.

He attends church with us now. In facing my fear of this boy, I acknowledge Christ's power and use my passion redemptively.

Becoming Redemptive Agents

Considering all of the evil that's out there, am I advocating that we run wildly into the streets, screaming a passionate and redemptive message to the gang members and drug dealers on every corner, grabbing guns and drug paraphernalia out of their hands as we pass?

Not exactly.

My experience with Eric taught me a lot about using my passion to stay safe as opposed to putting my energy into redemptively loving my world—my world being whomever God puts in my path on a given day.

How can I as a "fortyish" woman living in the suburbs consistently confront my fear and embrace the opportunity to passionately love my world? How can you?

The first step involves knowing what God's called you to—fear or passion. Fear will come; we can't avoid it. We must choose to confront our fear and embrace passion throughout our lives. This is God's intention for us. "I have come that they may have life, and have it to the full" (John 10:10). Passion is His intention.

So, if I know God's called me to passion, and furthermore, passionate redemption, the next step is choosing to act on that calling. Eric and my daughter broke up, and crazy as it seems, I still feel called to passionately love this child. The night they broke up, he came over to our house sobbing. He was facing a deep loss, not just the loss of his relationship with my daughter, but the loss of a family who cared about him.

"I love coming over to your house," he wailed. "I'm losing everything."

"We still want you in our lives," I told him and sincerely meant it.

If Eric ever becomes heavier than I can carry, I'll know that I'm supposed to direct my passion elsewhere. Today, I'm choosing to exercise my privilege of passionate loving to this person.

Once we decide to follow our calling to passionately love our world, whatever that means for each day, opportunities to express our individual gifts and abilities seem to drop into our laps.

For a number of years, I worked on various church boards with various women's groups. I taught women's Bible studies, spoke at women's groups, and organized women's retreats. That all abruptly stopped a few years ago. My passion now is drawn to children like Eric. When I saw a notice in the newspaper recently for a new group starting, I was the first one in the door. The group is called *Mothers Against Violence in America*. I care passionately about the violence perpetrated against children.

The point is, where is our passion taking us? The real question for each of us to answer is: "What is driving us to act—fear or passion?" If we are driven by fear, our actions will produce more fear. But if we are driven by a passionate response to God's calling, our actions will produce redemption in people's lives.

———

THREE

▼

PASSION BANDITS

$\mathbb{D}$ad, Dad!" said the young teenage boy as he charged into the house one evening, overflowing with his news. "I made five baskets tonight! Five! We won 64 to 59."

The father turned slowly in his chair at the dining room table where he sat writing out his monthly donation checks to various religious organizations.

"When you get as excited about winning souls as you do about making baskets, then I'll jump up and down with you," he said as he returned to his checks.

That boy never again tried to tell his father how many baskets he made at a game. The father never attended any of his son's games because there was always church, or ministry, or prayer meeting. I know this father and his son, and this is only one example of how this father robs his son of passion. It happens regularly.

In all honesty, every one of us, me included, is guilty at one time or another of holding others back from the passionate edge. What a terrible crime—to steal the life from someone's soul.

Later in this chapter, we'll discuss what it means to be a passion prodder, encouraging others to risk moving closer and closer to the edge. However, we can't be passion prodders for others unless we know how to protect our own passion from those who would try to steal it.

We can only protect our passion when we are able to recognize how others sabotage or victimize us, causing us to expend all of our energy protecting what's rightfully ours. Once we learn to recognize the signs of passion robbing, we no longer have to focus on self-protection. We often find it's as easy as removing ourselves from a situation or confronting our passion robber.

Exactly who are these passion robbers? Sadly, they're too often those closest to us.

Coworkers

If you work full-time, you spend eight or more hours a day with any number of coworkers. People you spend that much time with are going to affect you, positively or negatively.

I remember Susie, a woman I worked with in an office setting for a couple of years. A typical day with her was as follows:

"Good morning, Susie," I greeted her as I walked into my office.

She looked at me in shock. "What did you say?"

A heaviness began to descend on me at that point. "I said, 'Good morning.' Nice day, huh?"

"Good morning? Yeah, right. It's pouring down rain, my car wouldn't start, and I think I have cancer. I can't swallow." Susie contracted a different disease each week.

"I'm sure sorry," I sat down at my desk and tried to work.

However, Susie's desk was only three feet away from mine and the rest of the day I jumped as she slammed the phone down and shut the drawers in her desk. She made loud sighs and stomped her feet whenever she crossed the room.

I spent many passionless days in that job because Susie was an angry person, and my goal became to survive her angry days. I don't hold my coworker totally responsible. I allowed this person to rob me of my passion because I felt responsible to fix her anger. I felt like I needed to respond compassionately every time she slammed a drawer or sighed. Many days I turned my chair all the way around so at least I couldn't see her frowning face, so I wouldn't feel responsible and could work.

Depressed coworkers aren't much better, but at least drawers don't slam; they roll slowly shut. Sighs aren't loud and clipped but long and mournful. There aren't stomping feet but shuffling. It doesn't really matter—I still feel responsible to make the person feel better.

The truth is, all I'm responsible for in my place of employment is to do the best job I can. Of course, in God's eyes, we are indeed our brother's keeper and another's pain should matter to us. None of us, however, has the right to demand that our personal pain be the highest priority in someone else's day.

Another all-consuming passion bandit I often see in the workplace is something I call the junior-high caste system, such as the tyrants, tattletales, and troublemakers. It's really irrelevant as to which category I fit. I will say that it's not in the basic make up of my personality to be a tyrant or tattletale. You can figure it out from there. Oh, there are also the tweeters who stay at their desks and chirp nicely when asked for an opinion. They're rather benign so I tend to overlook them.

The power struggles that result as this system plays itself out are enough to make one want to climb into bed in the middle of the day. The tyrants run around giving orders in booming voices; the tattletales run around whining about the troublemakers; the troublemakers run around causing crises; and the tweeters run around in the vicinity of their desks, chirping loudly and pretending not to see anything the tyrants, tattletales, or troublemakers are doing. It's all quite exhausting.

If you're self-employed at home, be grateful. If you didn't spend too many years working in the junior-high caste system, your sanity may actually be intact.

Many specific passion-robbing workplace scenarios come to mind, more than I can describe on these pages. The important questions for you to ask are these: Are you growing in passion at your present place of employment? Do you look forward to going to work and interacting with your coworkers? Can you be creative, adventuresome, risk-taking? Or does loyalty, endurance, and faithfulness have your entire attention these days? Don't get me wrong—I believe in loyalty, endurance, and faithfulness. However, when we find ourselves focusing on them, it may be because we're settling instead of confronting or moving. Settling for something far beneath the abundant, fulfilling, and passionate life that God promises.

If you can be your passionate self in the midst of your boss and coworkers, congratulations. If they're cheering your walk on the edge, thank the Lord for where He's placed you.

But if, in thinking through your answers to those questions, you have any doubt at all that those people with whom you spend so many hours each day are *for* you and your commitment to passion, then you might want to consider a confrontation or move.

Take care of yourself. Don't settle for less than God's best.

Friends, Neighbors, and Other Enemies

For the most part, I have wonderful friends and neighbors who support me in my pursuit of passion. But over the years I've run into some real stinkers, and those are the ones we want to discuss.

In our discussion of passion bandits, what is there to say about our friends? Being honest, if I feel a person is robbing me of passion, I no longer count that person among my friends. A passion bandit might be an acquaintance or a neighbor, but a friend? I don't think so.

▼

I became suspicious that my "friend" Debbie, might be a passion bandit when too often she made comments like: "Be careful." "Watch out." "You don't really want to do that, do you?"

No matter in which direction I decided to fly, I felt her slam on the brakes before I even launched.

I confronted her a few times, but nothing changed. I began to see how full of fear she was, especially when it came to relational risks. Worst of all, not only did she put the brakes on me (and others, I discovered), but she actually tried to control my passionate ventures through manipulation. Coincidentally, she began to turn up everywhere, and I could always sense her watching me.

It became too much. I felt relief only when she was out of my life. If you're wondering how you get someone like this out of your life, it's not easy. By the way, I'm not really that harsh and callous—I don't go around kicking people out of my life for no reason.

When you begin to sense that a "friend" isn't for you because he or she has a personal agenda for your life, one that includes watching you closely in order to nab you when you fall off the edge, all in the name of "love," look again. Is this relationship good for you? Is it good for the other person? Are you enabling?

There are times I've been able to confront this issue in a friendship; the other person has heard; and we've remained friends, growing in the process. So, how do you confront someone who's attempting to rob your passion, keep you far from the passionate edge, and/or generally drain you of energy that could be used more productively somewhere else? You can't just walk up and say something like, "You're robbing me of my passion. Stop it."

When we're fed up with or resentful of someone, we usually tend to give off nonverbal signals. The other person doesn't often know how to read these signals or interprets the signals to mean something they don't. Hurt feelings ensue.

Sometimes this can't be helped. We just know it would be too hurtful to the other person to come right out and say what the problem is.

I have a friend who exhausts me with her constant chatter. For as much as she chatters is as much as I listen. Listening is hard work when there's no give and take in a conversation. What could I say to her? "You talk too much. I'm worn out."

No, instead, I avoid her. This woman has many other wonderful qualities, but I can't be around her too often.

What we must ask when evaluating a friendship for its life-giving or lack of life-giving qualities is: What kind of a relationship do I want with this person? Can we both benefit from a close friendship or is it better for us to remain acquaintances?

Awareness is the key. Too many times we stumble into friendships unconsciously and find ourselves in terribly uncomfortable situations because we've been caught off guard. Every relationship should make us more aware—aware of what we need and what we have to give.

Think about all of your friends. Which ones drain you? Which ones energize you? Which ones not only push you toward the edge, but dance along the edge with you? These are the kinds of friends to keep close.

Parents and Other Relatives

I walked slowly around my mother's hospital room, enjoying her many cards, flowers, and other gifts.

"Mom, so many people love you," I said, trying to be cheerful. She was in the last stage of ovarian cancer, and I had long ago run out of things to be cheerful about. "Look at all of these cards and flowers."

"Oh, I know," she groaned, waving a hand of dismissal. "What am I supposed to do with all of those flowers? I don't even know how I'll get them all home. I'll have to throw half of them out." She paused for a laborious breath. "My friends . . . they come in and line up against the wall with long faces. They're always crying. It's depressing."

I stared at my mother. Being a negative person, she couldn't even see or feel her friends' love for her in her final hours on earth. Suddenly, I felt so very sorry for her.

I'd always found it difficult being around my mother. She viewed life in various shades of black and gray. When days and weeks went by between visits, I didn't really miss her. Tragically, I realize now, she had been unhappy much of her life.

Yet, she had many good friends because in spite of her negativism, she did have a sense of humor. She could be a lot of fun. Her friends only saw her once in a while. They hadn't lived with her. Most importantly, they didn't need her the way I did.

This woman had given me physical life, and I needed her to give me emotional life, believe in me, push me toward the edge, and be proud of me. I needed her to live a passionate life and pass her passion on to me. However, as long as I'd known her, she'd stayed locked up tight, letting no one in.

When my mother died three weeks after that significant moment in her hospital room, I began to grieve and didn't stop for two months. I grieved everything that could have been and never was.

Many of my friends have moms and dads who cheer them and infuse them with passion every time they come around. These parents gave life to their children once, and they continue to give it over and over again by their very presence.

We are reluctant to talk negatively about our parents. We feel guilty because we know they did the best they could. They loved us the best they knew how. But if we're honest with ourselves, the best they knew how sometimes wasn't good enough. Sometimes it was far from good. Tragically, sometimes it wasn't good at all.

To move down the road toward the passionate edge, we have to face, acknowledge, and deal with what our parents didn't give us and what they may even be attempting to take from us now in our adulthood.

One fabulous thing to my mother's credit was that she may have lived far from the passionate edge herself, unable to express her feelings, but she never took my passion away from me when I was a child. I don't ever remember her telling me not to cry, be mad, or shut up.

Maybe unconsciously she did push me toward the passionate edge. By letting me have my feelings, she encouraged me to be me. That's the most direct way to real passion—expressing yourself as you are at any given moment.

John Bradshaw tells us in his book *Homecoming:* "What you feel at any given moment is the core of your authentic reality at that moment. Your inner child has had its feelings so bound with toxic shame that to feel *anything* is to feel toxic shame."[1]

I wasn't shamed for my feelings until I got married and by that time I had already reached "the core of my authentic reality" many times over, thanks to my mother.

How is it with your parents? They gave you life once. Are they giving you life now? Stay aware. This is how we grow. Take charge of your passionate self.

Children

How can children, those beautiful toddlers and teenagers, gifts from God, rob us of passion? If you're a parent and honest with yourself, you have to admit that parenting takes energy—at times, more energy than we have.

I was only twenty-two when the first of my five children was born. I had more energy than I could expend in a day—the pure physical energy that comes with youth. For years, while raising my five children, I was head of the nursery department at church, working with children during all of the three services every week and at extra meetings as well. Eventually I used up this physical energy. I collapsed before my children even reached their teen years.

When physical energy is all you have, it doesn't last forever. True physical passion, the kind of passion we need for parenting, must be fueled by genuine spiritual and emotional passion.

We can't blame our children for robbing us of our passion. They certainly don't do it on purpose. They just are, by their very nature, demanding creatures.

I have one child who has required all of my attention every day of her life. We are now discussing this, both of us acknowledging that this isn't fair, to me or my other children. One major factor is that she's been clinically depressed much of her life. She's simply been unable to cope. She's on medication now, and it's helping.

Raising one child is a full-time job. I have five, and for the last ten years, I've been a single parent. The overwhelming sense of responsibility I carry with me constantly seems heavier than I can bear. Because I want to maintain not only my passion but my sanity, I have to take care of myself. So do you.

One way I've done this over the years is to trade children with other mothers who need a break, just as I do. For a while, every mother I met was a potential kid-trader.

"I have a couple of kids who aren't in school yet, and I was wondering if you'd be interested in trading one day a week. I take your two on Thursday, and you take mine on Friday," I would say. To this day, no one has turned me down.

We don't have to ask whether it's God's will that we dispense much of our energy raising our children. If God's given them to us, it's His will. I also don't believe He wants to kill us in the process.

It was so freeing the day I realized that while I loved my children, I didn't enjoy being their mom all the time. It was hard, tiring, and painful. *These are normal feelings*, I tell myself as I head for the lake for yet another breathing space. *It's OK. I'll come back.* And I always do.

Spouse

Earlier I mentioned that we are hesitant to talk negatively about our parents. I've noticed this goes for our spouses, as well. We want to protect our image.

As Christians, we have a lot at stake. We tend to judge each other on the externals, and to admit we have less than perfect marriages is to admit that something is wrong with us. So we go on for years in our lives of pretense, often not even admitting to ourselves that everything is not right.

Many people believe that we are to esteem marriage above all else, that the goal is always to save the marriage, no matter what. No matter that individuals are kicked around. No matter that individuals are beating up on each other, physically and verbally. No matter that individuals are dying.

I happen to believe that Jesus died on the cross, not for marriages, but for individuals. That's not to say that we are to take marriage lightly. One reason I'm not married today, ten years after my divorce, is because I take it very seriously. I choose not to put my passion into that kind of relationship at this point in my life, when I'm raising my children and working at a job that demands so much from me already.

I know God highly honors the marriage commitment. But when the institution that God ordained brings death instead of life, something's wrong.

Separating from a spouse is the last resort. The truth about marriage is that it takes two people to make it work. I know one counselor who tells his women clients that it only takes one—the woman, of course. What pressure!

For those brave souls who are willing to admit that the marriage is taking much more out of them than it's giving, a step in itself that brings one closer to the passionate edge, there is definitely hope.

The spouse who robs our passion is the alcoholic, the two-timer, the abusive spouse who seems to take delight in making another person miserable.

It doesn't really take the extreme to rob us of our passion. It could simply be the insecure mate who demands a bit more than we have to give in the emotional arena. It could be a physically handicapped mate for whom we are the major caregiver. It could be a mate who's in a mid-life crisis.

For whatever reason, our spouse, our lover for life, is draining us of energy, keeping us far from the abundant life that Jesus promised. If this is true for you, what, if anything, can you do? Everyone's situation is so different, no easy answers come to mind, but you must do something. Passion, in individuals and in relationships, doesn't stop dying all by itself.

You've got to find a way to turn it around. Not just so that your spouse will no longer drain you of your personal passion, but so that your heart will once again leap when that person walks into the room, smiles at you, or climbs into bed beside you—so that you're once again excited about growing old with that person.

It's definitely worth putting your passion into.

Who am I to talk about marriage when mine failed? I'm an authority on everything not to do in marriage. I vowed I'd never write about marriage and here I am, but I can't talk about passion without some kind of discussion on this most important union between two people. For those of you who are married, the kind of relationship you have with your spouse is key to how much passion you have toward life, in how you view life, and in how you participate in life.

The most important questions for you at this time are: Is your marriage giving you life or draining it from you? Does your spouse excite you or unnerve you?

If, in answering these questions, you realize that one reason you have little passion is because of what your marriage is taking out of you, what can you do about it? My prayer for you is that the following chapters will indeed provide you with some insights that will not only ignite your personal passion, but will infuse your relationship with your spouse, as well.

Passion Prodders

I'll never forget the little woman who sat in the front row at church and played the kazoo during worship. Stringy, long blonde hair bounced from side to side as she moved her head in time to the music, her foot tapping, and her body swaying. I could hear that annoying, flat honking sound a kazoo makes—at least a kazoo that's played by someone who hasn't a clue as to how to play a kazoo.

Fortunately, my husband and I always sat toward the back of the church. That way, we weren't able to hear the honking as well as some of the "front-seaters."

No one ever ushered her out. No one ever asked her to leave her kazoo at home or in her lap. No one ever said anything at all.

Many times after the service she'd stand in line along with the rest of us to talk to the pastor. She sat in the front row and was always first in line. I guessed she might be hard of hearing because she talked so loudly. Probably one reason she played the kazoo so loudly was she couldn't hear herself.

The amazing thing was that our pastor listened to her ramble on and on about whatever was exciting her that day. Oh yes, she was always passionate about something. He actually acted interested, not only interested but totally engaged, like no one else was in the room.

One time she brought a puppet to church. For once the annoying kazoo sounds were absent during worship. However, I'm not sure we were any better off because above everyone's heads, the curly-haired puppet, an animated fellow, nodded and shook his head as appropriate during our pastor's sermon.

After the service, we lined up as usual to talk to our pastor and waited patiently as he conversed with the puppet.

"Yes, it's a nice day," our pastor remarked to the puppet. "I'm so glad you enjoyed my sermon."

Yes, the kazoo and puppet were annoying. Yes, it was irritating waiting in line for her to go on and on about nothing, but I decided that day that our pastor was as close to who Jesus is as anyone I'd ever met in my life.

I don't know where that woman is today or if she's still talking about kazoos and puppets. However, I know she'll never find anyone more supportive, more encouraging, or more interested in her "silly" little passions as our pastor. I want to be just like him.

What my pastor did for that young woman, he did for everyone. If something was important to someone, no matter what it was, it was important to him. Not only was he not a passion robber, he was and is a passion prodder.

You may be someone's boss or coworker. You're most certainly someone's friend and neighbor. Maybe you're a parent. You're definitely someone's child. And very possibly you're someone's spouse. In each of these roles, are you supporting and cheering others in their pursuits of passion?

———

FOUR

▼

WAKING UP

How does it feel to wake up? Journalist Anna Louise Strong describes the waking up process like this: "It was as if I had worked for years on the wrong side of a tapestry, learning accurately all its lines and figures, yet always missing its color and sheen."[1]

Viewing the wrong side of a tapestry reveals a maze of tangled and crisscrossed threads. If we never turned the tapestry over, we would think that this was all there was, and we'd wonder, "Where's the beauty, the reward for our labor, the design?"

The apostle Paul put it like this: "When I was a child, I talked like a child, I thought like a child, I reasoned like a child. When I became a man, I put childish ways behind me. . . . Now I know in part; then I shall know fully, even as I am fully known" (1 Cor. 13:11–12b).

To put childish ways behind us is to turn the tapestry over. Some believe that to know fully is to have all knowledge once we're in heaven. I'm not a theologian, but I believe we can begin to know fully down here—by turning the tapestry over and approaching the passionate edge.

The First Stirrings

If I could have one wish for those of you moving toward the passionate edge, it would be that the first inner stirrings of life would be pleasant ones, so that you'd keep moving forward.

Unfortunately, wishing doesn't make it so. Some of us stir awake to awesome feelings of wonder, pleasure, and joy. Others of us to awesome feelings of torment, agony, and pain. Sometimes it's a combination. If we're old enough, mature enough, and knowledgeable enough, the transition is manageable—at least bearable.

At thirty-two, I was young, immature, and ignorant; the process of waking up was neither manageable nor bearable. At forty-two, it was neither manageable nor bearable for Jackie. She disappeared.

Jackie was a coworker of ours, someone we all liked. She had a smile and kind word for everyone. She was dependable, intelligent, and mature—we thought. As a single woman for a number of years, she owned her own home, wore nice clothes, and drove a nice car.

Her nice car was found abandoned by the police in a movie-theater parking lot. Upon inspection, her nice clothes were found still hanging in the closet at her nice home. Jackie had vanished.

Was she abducted? That had to be the case. There was no other possible explanation.

Poor Jackie. Those of us who worked with her could think of nothing else. Was she being tortured somewhere? Held against her will? Dead? For weeks we wondered.

One day, a month later, Jackie called. Our nice, sweet, mature coworker had run away. Why? In an effort to escape,

▼

silence, and beat down those first stirrings, she'd gone over the edge.

We all felt guilty. Could we have prevented this somehow? Weren't there signs? How could we have helped our friend?

We might have prevented it. There may or may not have been signs. We might have been able to help Jackie, but we might not. It all depended on how awake we ourselves were. You can only offer solutions when you can see a problem. You can only see signs if you're awake. You can only lead a blind person if you yourself can see.

Upon Jackie's return, she entered counseling and began to deal with those first inner stirrings that caused her to lose control. Jackie's return to reality woke us all up.

We began to relate heart to heart. Instead of "Good morning," we started talking to each other, hearing each other, seeing each other, and caring for each other.

In the long run, some of those affected by Jackie's experience returned to business as usual. They had danced dangerously close to the passionate edge and changed their minds.

But others of us will never be the same. It has definitely helped me put my own waking-up process in perspective (I give myself much more grace now) as well as changed the way I relate to others in their first stirrings of wakefulness.

I'm much more patient with those who, in their first stirrings, act a little crazy. I'm choosing to validate their feelings instead of condemning their behavior. Validating their feelings enables them to, in their own time, look at their behavior. I'm willing to allow them some crazy behavior in order to help bring forth the real persons God created.

Jackie paid a high price in front of all of us, but I'm grateful that I *saw* her and *saw* what God was doing.

It's scary, this relating heart to heart and really seeing one another. Without understanding what it all means, nearing the passionate edge sends the message that: (1) We must take responsibility for our lives—it's a trade-off; we receive the gift of freedom if we can also give the gift of responsibility.

(2) We must confront and deal with the pain that grows more intense the closer we draw to the edge; we receive the gift of feelings if we are willing to accept the pain along with the joy. (3) We are created for and to love; we receive the gift of love if we can deny our own comfort when that's what God requires.

I think God planned it this way. How many of us would honestly run for the passionate edge if we knew ahead of time everything that would be required of us? I, for one, know what my response would have been had the next few years' agenda been laid out for me: "No thanks. I'll just stay here where it's less intense."

What kinds of strange stirrings have you felt recently? Could something be trying to wake you up? How are you responding?

I remember one of the first stirrings I felt was lust. How humiliating. Here I was an old, married woman with five children. How could this be happening?

I hadn't had a truly lustful thought since high school fifteen years before. However, this wasn't because I was so pure or righteous, I soon realized, but because I was dead.

No, I'm not saying you'll feel lust when you start to wake up, or that you *should* feel lust when you start to wake up. But, to be honest, you may get a few surprises. Some of them, in fact, are quite wonderful.

Surprises

I woke up one morning, looked out our front window, and saw the plum tree budding bright pink blossoms in the front yard. We'd lived there five years. Had the tree never blossomed before? Or had I never noticed?

I put an album on the stereo and heard music—not noise, but violins, trumpets, guitars, flutes, and pianos. Each note rang out, clear and harmonious. It made me happy. Something was happening. It was a new day.

My children did the same things they did every day—spilled their juice, hit each other, messed up the house. Now these things provoked a strange inner stirring—anger.

A teenage friend died of a brain tumor. My husband said, "Rejoice! She's in heaven," and went about his day. I felt something else, something far from joy. This strange stirring could only be called sadness, grief, and sorrow. I was alive!

Everyone was so shocked when President Carter admitted he had lustful thoughts from time to time. I remember thinking, *What's the big deal? What's everyone so upset about? The man's being honest. Such honesty should be applauded.*

Life on the passionate edge includes uncomfortable thoughts and feelings sometimes. The devil took Jesus into the wilderness to tempt Him. We can read in thirty seconds the Bible's account of this crucially important event in Jesus' life. Satan spent forty days pulling everything out of his bag of tricks. We really don't know all that went on. The Bible doesn't give us all the specifics. We do know that He was "tempted in *every* way, just as we are—yet was without sin" (Heb. 4:15).

I don't know about you, but watching everyone's response to Jimmy Carter only taught me that we don't talk about our struggles. The devil doesn't play favorites—everyone is tempted with lust of all kinds. I've deduced that the people who think they are never tempted to lust possibly aren't alive. And because they're not alive they approach life quite simply—they know exactly what's right and what's wrong. It's easy for these folks to do right because there's no struggle. Dead people don't struggle. Therefore, it's also easy for these folks to point self-righteous fingers at those who do struggle.

A few years ago, I hadn't figured any of this out, so when those lustful thoughts hit, they took me completely by surprise. I was riding my bike, minding my own business when out of the blue, I saw this guy.

Of course, I didn't dare tell a soul. What would I say? That all of this time I thought I was a saint, and now I found out I was really a rotten sinner after all? I didn't even acknowledge

▼

this lust to myself. I was mortified, so I told myself it must have been something I ate and went on with my day.

I usually like surprises, but these surprises were so surprising that I wasn't sure I liked them at all.

I mean, what are we supposed to do with sudden awakening feelings? At that time, all of the Christian books simply said: No, you're not supposed to have feelings. Get rid of them fast.

We can succeed in doing that for a while. We pretend those feelings aren't there. If we ignore them, they'll go away. If you do succeed in making them go away for any length of time, you endanger your soul—they may be gone for good and the passionate edge will be lost to you. You may never have to worry again about being surprised by passion.

God gives us that choice. But we tend to take the easy way out. We don't like things to get too complicated. Life on the passionate edge is definitely complicated—less black and white, lots of gray, less certainty and more confusion.

The nature of life on the passionate edge demands that we not repress these feelings but learn to deal with them in a healthy and redemptive way.

Longings Awakened

In his book, *Inside Out*, Dr. Larry Crabb says:

We are thirsty people. We long for:

a. physical comfort (casual longings);

b. good relationships with people (critical longings);

c. the joys that only relationship with God provides (crucial longings).[2]

One of the first things that happens when we begin to wake up is that we touch our longings.

I have never quite figured out if the abandonment feelings I suffer from time to time are because of parental neglect in my childhood or because I'm a human being. All I know is that when I felt the first stirrings of life, one of these feelings was intense aloneness.

I was on a plane recently waiting for it to crash, and it wasn't even snowing. When I'm in the air, I'm somehow keenly aware that what goes up must come down. If I come down too hard, that's called a plane crash, and passengers in plane crashes often die. So, I was waiting to die, but since it wasn't happening yet, I had some time to think about why I always thought about this.

I pictured the crash like I always do and then something suddenly dawned on me. I thought, *Why, if I go down, all of these other folks are going with me.* I looked around at my fellow passengers. A businessman sat on my right, busily typing away on his laptop computer. On the other side of him, a young woman snoozed. Across the aisle sat a husband and wife with a small boy between them playing some kind of card game. Everyone seemed completely oblivious to the fact that we were miles above the ground and our collective deaths were imminent. However, this wasn't what struck me. All I knew was that I wasn't alone on this plane. I was immediately comforted and fell asleep, exhausted by all of my anxiety.

It's not death I'm afraid of—it's dying *alone*. The idea of going through that particular life transition by myself makes me a little crazy. I want to be with someone.

In this chapter we've talked about surprises. Those first longings are quite surprising, to say the least. Before waking up, we may think we know ourselves. The new longings we experience upon waking feel foreign and strange. Suddenly you may feel lonely in your marriage. You long to know your spouse more deeply. You long for more closeness in your family.

I woke up to new longings for my mother, to whom I'd never been close, and my father who had died when I was five. Many of my deep inner longings went back to childhood.

What do we do with these longings? Obviously, we can't get all of them fulfilled. We lack understanding of what's happening and so we may too quickly reach out to satisfy what we may think of as "cravings" with the nearest fix—an affair, a drink, another church service. Yes, some of us even use church as an anesthetic. Rather than feel the uncomfortableness of unfulfilled longings, we run from church service to church service in an effort to fill the void.

But these longings, these new feelings, mean something. They mean something unique to each of us because we are all unique persons. Our challenge is to find out what they mean about who we're becoming in the Kingdom of God.

We must learn to quit running, to stand perfectly still and feel the longing, and to turn to God for comfort and direction in this place. He will comfort us in our longing and direct us to what to do with it: (1) find a healthy way to fulfill it, or (2) live with it, or (3) grieve it and let it go. The goal is always growth. We want to keep moving steadily forward in our pursuit of the passionate edge.

Forward Movement

The beginning of the journey in passion reminds me of the first driving lessons my mother gave me. I sat behind the wheel, feeling the power of the engine in our 1963 Chevy at my fingertips, or foottips—a little pressure from my right foot and we were off. For at least ten feet. Ooomph, ooomph, ooomph, ooomph, ooomph. Funny, our car had never acted this jerky before.

"Stop!" my mother screamed.

I slammed on the brakes, sending my mother sprawling against the door. That was OK. She'd been practically on my lap ever since we'd left the driveway.

"What's the problem?" I asked.

She glared at me, checked for blood and bruises, then slid over next to me again. She gripped the dashboard with both hands, as if we were in a rocket rather than a 1963 Chevy. "Let's try it again," she bravely commanded.

I let up on the clutch and pressed on the gas. Ooomph, ooomph, ooomph!

"Stop!" my mother screamed. And so it went until I learned to drive.

The beginning of the journey toward passion is jerky because we're not sure what we're supposed to do. Even if someone tells us, we're not sure how to do it. Some of the blunders we make are as embarrassing as jerking down the street in a1963 Chevy, my mother on my lap, the whole neighborhood watching. I've had more people than I can count screaming "Stop!" at me as I bumble along.

I remember a scene from the movie *Dead Poets Society.* More than anything in the world, Neil Perry wanted to be an actor. Finally, his big opportunity arrived. He was chosen to play an important part in a community play. There was only one problem—he needed his father's permission, but Perry wasn't deterred. He ran into the room he shared with Todd Anderson at Welton Academy, screaming, "I got the part! I got the part!"

"What?" Anderson asked from his corner of the room where he was studying. "What part?"

"I got the part in the play," said Perry.

Anderson just stared at him curiously. "You can't do that. You know your dad . . ."

"I'm going to do it!" Perry challenged. "I'm going to do this!"

"Neil, you're crazy. Your dad will never let you do it and you know it," said Anderson.

Suddenly, Perry "heard" him and his face fell. "OK. OK . . . but, I mean, can't I even enjoy the feeling for a while?"

Perry was jerking down the street, trying hard to follow his passion, but someone was always there screaming, "Stop!" Those someones won't even allow us to enjoy the feelings for a while. How can we make any real progress if we're listening to everyone on the sidelines scream, "Stop!"?

I was absolutely determined to learn how to drive. It meant freedom, after all. Perry was absolutely determined to be an actor, so determined that when his father said no he immediately felt trapped and decided to commit suicide rather than not be able to pursue his passion. This is a good lesson for all those who would try to stop another person from pursuing the passionate edge. We have a lot of influence over one another.

We must be determined, so determined, that for us there is no turning back, no matter who is screaming at us.

No Turning Back

I saw a cartoon once. A young husband was helping his very pregnant wife who was obviously in labor up the steps of the hospital. The caption underneath said, "Are you sure you want to go through with this?"

That's exactly how we must look at this journey in passion. Once on the journey, we can't look for escape hatches. We may feel like we aren't making progress all of the time, but that's OK.

Every once in a while I get on one of those wild carnival rides, and, just as it starts, I panic. *I think I've just changed my mind about this ride,* I say to myself. *I think I'd like to get off now.* The ride is accelerating, and we're going faster and higher, but it's too late. I can't change my mind. I might as well relax and enjoy the ride.

I've seen people turn back from the passionate edge, and they're some of the most miserable people I know. It just doesn't work. I can't even imagine going back to the person I was before.

So what this means is that you need to be sure of what you want before you get too far into it, because you can't ever really go home again. It's sometimes wilder than the wildest carnival ride. It can go higher than the highest plane, faster than the fastest jet. It's like life on a different planet compared to what you've known. Your past life only resembles a corpse, and once you see it for what it is, you can't help but recoil.

You've made a choice. Keep going.

———

FIVE

▼

NEW FEELINGS

Has anyone ever said to you, "You're too sensitive." Have you ever spoken those words to someone else? At some time or another we've probably all said this, usually because we don't know how to respond to someone else's intense emotion. So we try to put the responsibility back on the other person.

There is one thing you will learn about living your life on the passionate edge, though; feelings of all kinds and intensities are everywhere. You can definitely begin to feel like you're being "too sensitive," reacting to everything and everyone. It's simply because you're no longer numb. You're finally alive.

So don't buy into the words, "You're too sensitive." It's a wonderful thing, this coming alive. It's not a matter of being too sensitive. It's a matter of learning how to manage the new feelings, to control them so that our passions can lead us to productive growth.

Awareness Awakening

Every move toward the passionate edge sharpens and fine tunes our sensitivity and level of awareness. When we choose to stay with the feeling, the passion, or the hard situation, we take a step closer.

I watched a friend do this recently. Four of my friends and I were out to dinner, and suddenly we were in a discussion none of us had planned.

"I can't quit my job," my friend told us. "I'm four years from retirement."

"But your heart's not there anymore," I reminded her. "You're watching the clock. Your body's there, but you're not. If you could be anywhere, where would you be?"

"With my grandchildren." Her eyes filled with tears. "I'd be back in Florida playing with my grandkids."

"Then that's where you need to be," I said.

"We don't have enough money," she said.

"You've got a savings account," I went on. "Hey, this is your life, remember. You only get to do this once."

"I don't know," she hesitated.

"Follow your passion!" I hissed louder than I'd intended. I wanted to stand on the table and scream it to the entire restaurant. My friend had no idea what she stood to lose if she denied her gut.

A few days later I received a note.

"I don't know when it will be, but I know I've got to go. I'll hate saying good-bye . . . " my friend wrote.

Me too. I'll hate saying good-bye, but when a person chooses to take the next step, we don't dare hang on. I applaud my buddy's courage.

I'd watched her struggle over this issue for years. I watched the struggle grow worse over time and her die inside. Just that night at dinner she'd said no at least fifty times before she'd said yes. In the end she listened to her heart. She let herself be awakened. Although there would be much pain in the move itself, we would watch it get better because she was facing her fear—she was terrified of not having enough money in her older years—and embracing her passion.

She'll always be more aware now. It won't be as easy for her to turn a deaf ear to that stirring inside that says: "Listen. Feel. Move." She'll recognize the call of the passionate edge and hopefully, she'll take the next step.

Our hearts speak to us often, more often than we listen. We must learn to recognize our hearts' voices. It's the voice of God. A heart committed to Him can trust its passion.

It's weird. You'd think the closer you move to the passionate edge, the more you'd understand about how it all works, the more settled you'd feel inside, and the more confident you'd grow.

That's why the confusion always takes us by surprise.

Confusion

"I want to do this. And I want to do that. And I wouldn't mind it if I could do this, too."

"I need to confront this, but I need to back off from that, I think. I should probably deal with this."

So what do I do? I don't know. Are we ever really sure? Of anything? I'm not sure where we pick up erroneous beliefs, convictions, and ideas, but they do seem to attach themselves to us along the Christian walk. Somewhere along the way we pick up the idea that to be confused is to sin. The "walk of faith," according to what we're taught, does not include confusion of any kind. If one is confused, it's because the devil is playing around somewhere close—as close as in our minds.

We think that to confess confusion is to confess the devil's working in our mind, so we never confess it. We seldom talk about it to each other. Of course, not talking about confusion doesn't mean we're never confused.

When you're gut level honest with yourself, do you always know exactly what to do how and when? Always? When you have two jobs to choose from? Two churches? Two people you're in love with?

I've watched talk shows where the audience is asked to imagine hypothetical situations and then imagine the moral decision they might make in the situation: If your child and husband or wife were both drowning and you could only save one, which would you choose? Would you rob a bank if you knew you'd never get caught? If you found the love of your life but he or she happened to be the brother or sister of your current fiancee, would you leave your fiancee for this person?

While I enjoy playing along, fantasizing what I'd do with a million dollars, I really think these shows are a little ridiculous. How often are we faced with these kinds of decisions in real life? I know life's confusing, but this is stretching it, isn't it? These kinds of things don't happen in reality . . . do they?

Well, when our family faced a dilemma recently, I wasn't at all prepared. If it was nothing else, it was definitely confusing. No clear cut answer presented itself. I couldn't find the answer in the Bible. God didn't write it in the sky (I looked), on tablets of stone, or even in my mind or heart that I could sense.

My teenage daughter, clinically depressed and often suicidal for most of her young life, started taking the controversial anti-depressant, Prozac, which made a huge difference in her emotional well-being. For the first time in her life, she had some self-esteem and genuinely liked herself. She even seemed happy at times. Then she came home one day and spoke the words every parent dreads: "I'm pregnant."

As if dealing with all of the ramifications of the pregnancy weren't enough, the immediate question became: "Will Prozac harm the fetus?" No one knew—not us, not the pharmacist, not even our psychiatrist.

Living on the passionate edge means a continual confronting of the hard questions, making decisions, trusting God for the outcome, and watching Him redeem when our decisions are less than His best.

In the past, I might have given it five seconds of thought and left her on Prozac, pretending I didn't know any better. I mean, we all had to live with her—there was our sanity to consider, after all. However, in the past I wouldn't have put my daughter on Prozac in the first place. I would have told her, "What's to be depressed about anyway? Count it all joy when you suffer."

Thank God living close to passion means responding in *com*passion to those around us who are hurting. If we can do anything at all to alleviate nonproductive and unnecessary suffering, we must do so. First, I considered that.

In laboratory tests, Prozac had had no effect on the fetuses of pregnant rats. But it was a new drug, and they were still researching the side effects. What if the baby was born retarded or deformed—we would always wonder. And this little person, even though we didn't know him or her yet, deserved every chance to live a productive life.

She agreed to give up Prozac.

Yes, my daughter has her down days, but just as mothers do, whether they're fifteen or forty-five, she's sacrificing her personal happiness for her unborn child—just in case. She's learning about the passionate edge, too—to go with her gut, hope for the best, and let God redeem the rest.

It's OK to be confused, to not know and be unsure.

Yes, living with confusion makes life more complicated. Confusion, however, doesn't have to be your enemy. As you near the passionate edge, you'll have many times of confusion. Make it your friend by embracing it, taking a tentative step, and watching God set you on solid ground.

Loneliness

Sometimes, as we move closer to the edge, we encounter loneliness. We are growing older and wiser, and it makes sense that we should have more of the answers to life. Yet, we seem to have more questions and fewer answers than ever before. But the really hard part is that we look at everyone else, and they seem to be moving merrily along in their lives, collecting more of the answers as they go—or so it seems. We often feel like we have more problems than ever; yet everyone else is getting their act together—or so it seems. We feel like we're standing still and everyone else is moving ahead—or so it seems.

The passionate edge is not a crowded place. In many ways, the journey there is a solitary one, but we're not at all prepared for the loneliness.

It's a walk of integrity. A walk that doesn't necessarily take into consideration everyone else's opinions, and since everyone loves to share their opinions (many actually consider this their mission in life), they don't take kindly to you if you are less than eager to listen. So they drop out of sight.

Sometimes the loneliness becomes so intense we sacrifice our integrity to hang out with the masses again, just so we won't feel so all alone. It never works, never feels quite right. We've ventured so close to the passionate edge. We feel the pull of what it might be like to live there, and we can't really go back to being part of the masses. After a point, retreating from the passionate edge means losing respect for oneself.

The closer Jesus drew to His crucifixion the less He was able to "win friends and influence people." There weren't many folks crowded around His cross. Even His good friend Peter denied he knew Him.

I would never claim to compare the purpose of the passionate edge to the purpose of the cross, yet some things are similar.

I can't imagine a lonelier time for any person in history than the moments our Lord spent on the cross. I think that Jesus had things pretty well mapped out before He came to planet Earth. Certainly the loneliness didn't take Him by surprise.

However, the loneliness took me by surprise. I thought I was traveling a well-populated road, not "the road less traveled"[1] as Scott Peck calls it. Unlike Jesus who was so gracious in His lonely moment—forgiving everyone, showing mercy to His crucifiers, making sure everyone was taken care of (connecting His mother and John the beloved)—I haven't been anything even close to gracious during my lonely times.

Now I'm learning that "lonely is OK," and it's not just OK, it's an important part of living on the passionate edge. I believe loneliness is not a feeling we should run from, but one to embrace as part of sharing in "the sufferings of Christ."

So, when sudden loneliness takes us by surprise, we don't have to panic. What is God saying? He always has something to teach us in our lonely feelings if we're watching and waiting. To find out what that is, we can do the following:

▼ Check out the surroundings—what sparked the feeling in the first place?

▼ Remember our spiritual journey—what's going on currently? (A lonely feeling may mean something different.)

▼ Pray for enlightenment—are we supposed to be doing anything different?

Being on the passionate edge we discover the unfamiliar feelings of confusion and loneliness that don't immediately go away with a quick fix like they used to. And if that's not hard enough, there comes an increasing restlessness.

Restlessness

I wonder if the restlessness we sometimes feel is due to the passionate edge's nearness to our eternal home. I suppose I'll never know for sure. All I do know for sure is that the restlessness seems to grow in intensity the longer we're on this path.

Before I understood it very well, I identified restlessness as discontent—or the need for a job change, a new group of friends, new clothes. Now I know it's part of the process.

What does it feel like? I need something. I can't get satisfied. I have to go somewhere, do something. Sometimes it's uncomfortable, sometimes it's frustrating.

If you're like me, you've been taught that Christians are supposed to have perfect peace. It even says that in the Bible: "You will keep in perfect peace him whose mind is steadfast, because he trusts in you" (Isa. 26:3). Therefore, if I don't have perfect peace, my mind must not be steadfast; I must not be trusting in the Lord.

I once tormented myself with this kind of guilt, but I struggle less with those kinds of Scriptures now. I know that God always holds out the ideal. Of course, He'd like me to be thinking about Him all of the time.

The point is that restlessness is nothing to be ashamed of. It doesn't mean something is spiritually wrong with us, that we're unstable or not trusting God. Actually, the restless times cause me to reach out and trust God in a way I don't have to when everything is sailing along. When I'm restless I know something is up—He's doing something and I want to be alert. It really helps if we can prepare ourselves for these times and expect them, just like we do the confusion and loneliness.

One reason it's important to understand the restlessness and expect it is because if we don't we may end up misinterpreting it as hunger and eat too much, or thirst and drink too much, or the need for intimacy and end up making all kinds of mistakes.

When we choose to live close to our passions, we'll experience restlessness because our passions involve everything we feel strongly about. Obviously, we can't go all day every day fulfilling our passions.

Jesus got to fulfill His passions all day every day because He was totally in touch with His Father. He and His Father were one. Their one overriding passion during the time Jesus walked the earth was to build the kingdom of God. Every one of Jesus' activities, whether it was feeding the hungry, healing the sick, or teaching His disciples, fell under His one passion—building the kingdom of God. I like to think I'm getting there, that my passions have more to do with kingdom building than they used to.

What is meant by kingdom building?

▼ Loving God and others,

▼ Developing the kinds of relationships that require both vulnerability and confrontation (so we can grow), and

▼ Modeling the character of Christ so that others will want to know Him.

I'm sure you could add your own kingdom building actions to the list.

The restlessness will always be there when humanly, our longings and passions go unfulfilled, and when spiritually, kingdom building isn't happening fast enough or in the way we think it should.

There's one more feeling that takes us by surprise as we near the passionate edge.

Cynicism and Intolerance

When I was still far away from touching my passionate self, I could feel a bitter cynicism creeping into my everyday attitude. This often happens when we're in pain and haven't yet found a way to resolve it.

Someone might say, "Oh, I'm just waiting for the man God has picked out for me. A good man."

A good man? Yeah, right. Don't hold your breath, I think.

Someone might say, "I've found the most wonderful church. They really care about people."

A wonderful church? Yeah, right. Just wait.

When we've hurt long and hard, we can't believe there's anything good that exists anywhere. Wait long enough and life will show its poisonous side. Because we've touched the deep places of pain, this kind of cynicism may actually increase as we move toward the passionate edge.

Don't be alarmed. When this happens, we must remind ourselves that good men *are* still out there. (If we're running into the psychos and freaks it may be because we're projecting our own bitterness and attracting the wrong kind of men.)

Yes, there are loving churches out there. (If we haven't found one, again, we must look inside. Am I, are you, the trouble-maker?)

I find myself often prefacing my comments on a subject with, "I may just be a cynic but . . . ." This is because it's usually easier for me to discredit my comments and opinions than it is for me to keep my mouth shut altogether. Or if I forget to preface my comments and just open my mouth and say whatever it is, I'll end my comments with, "That may just be my cynical side coming out."

It's unrealistic, if we live in reality, to think we can actually escape having a cynical side of any kind, but we can learn how to temper it and even have fun with it without hurting people. One way to do this is to become more tolerant.

You'd think that the more aware we become the more tolerant we'd be, but the opposite is true. The more enlightened we become, the easier it is to lose patience with those still in the dark. We wish they would hurry up, grow up, and wake up, so they wouldn't be so annoying in their unenlightenment, so dull in their ability to see truth, and so slow to comprehend the passionate life. I hate to admit it, but the closer we come to the passionate edge, the more arrogant we tend to be.

The point is don't be surprised when this happens for it will happen. It's another of Satan's ploys to render us ineffective. If he can't keep us from the passionate edge, he can at least cause us to think we're better than others so that we will end up separated from the people of God, silenced, alone in our indi-viduality.

One way I handle my cynicism and intolerance is to make a joke out of it. That way no one will take me too seriously, and I won't hurt anyone.

I have little tolerance for fanatical religious types. One time I told one person that I thought another person was too relig-ious. The first person agreed with me. Adding my opinion to hers to use as ammunition, the first person told the second what I'd said about him. First, he refused to talk to me. Then when

▼

he did, he said, "I heard you think I'm too religious. I don't appreciate you saying—"

"Hold it," I interrupted. "You already know I think you're too religious. That's not even news."

He didn't know what to say when I admitted it so fast. "Well . . . well . . . I don't think it's a problem. You said it was a problem,"he said.

"I do think it's a problem," I said. "Oh well, we all have problems, don't we?" We just laughed and changed the subject.

I knew I was in trouble the minute we started the conversation. I didn't want to come off as intolerant nor did I want to be intolerant. Because I value my relationship with this person more than I need to state my opinions about his religious state of being, I knew I had to get out of this somehow, so I made it no big deal.

What's hard to take are obnoxious cynics and intolerant bigots who no one wants to be around because they're always putting down an individual or a group for something they don't agree with. It's usually not for any good reason, simply a personal bias.

As you near the passionate edge, one of the feelings that may surprise you is your tendency to be intolerant and cynical. Don't worry too much about it. Just remember to keep it light. If you have a sense of humor, there's always a way out.

The passionate edge is full of new feelings. That's one of the things I love about it. Your feelings have a lot to teach you. Eventually you'll get used to acknowledging them as they surface, and the challenge will become not to try to get rid of them, but to look at them so that you might learn something about yourself and your journey in passion.

Hang on. When you're in touch with your passion, you never know what's around the corner in the way of new feelings and ways of expressing them.

S I X

▼

SAYING GOOD-BYE

I quit."

My boss looked up from the pile of papers on her desk and said, "What?"

"I quit. I'm quitting. I'm, uh, giving notice," I repeated.

"Well, when were you thinking? I mean . . ."

Her usual smooth demeanor was a little shaken. I'd taken her by surprise. That was OK. I'd surprised myself. I hadn't really known until an hour before that today was the day I would actually do it.

Oh, I knew it was coming. I'd known for at least a year, and what a year it was—one of struggle, great turmoil, and soul searching. I'd worked there seven years; but for a number of reasons, I knew it was time to move on. It's just that I'd always assumed that another job, the perfect job, would present itself before I quit. It would be the sign that I was to leave.

It never happened, and here I was quitting without another job to go to, no savings account, no unemployment—nothing.

Everyone said I was crazy. A co-worker went home and told her husband what I'd done.

"Isn't she the one with the five kids?" her husband asked.

A nod.

"Shouldn't she have gotten another job before she quit?"

Of course that is the way sane, rational, normal, and mature people do things. It's just that I've never been particularly sane, rational, or normal (whatever that is), and certainly not mature.

But I've always believed in seizing the day. I sensed it was time to go. So I went.

I'm not suggesting that we follow every whim we receive from who knows where any old time of any old day. But in this particular instance I chose to trust my gut feeling and follow my passion, no matter how stupid my decision looked to others, no matter how bad the timing seemed to be, and no matter how scary this step toward the edge was for me.

It's almost as if the passionate edge was calling me, beckoning me, crying out to me to come.

Now or not at all, that's what drove me into my boss' office that day. Scarier than not having a job, scarier than not having money, and scarier than people thinking I was stupid and impulsive was the possibility that I might miss the opportunity to follow my passion. Because I was at that time in the process of learning to shut out the outside voices and trust the internal voice of God inside me.

Something had been stirring for about a year. Suddenly I knew if I didn't let go, I couldn't move ahead. It was now or not at all.

Instinctively I knew that if I didn't quit my job that day, I never would. Then I'd never discover the new adventure I felt stirring inside. I'd miss the opportunity for growth. Most importantly, I'd trade my passion for security. No way.

These are difficult, gut-wrenching, internally tormenting times. Easy answers elude us, although everyone has opinions: "You can't do that. It's stupid." "But you've never done that before." "Look what you're risking."

What about what we risk if we don't do it? We risk staying asleep, forfeiting the daring adventure Helen Keller talks about, and losing sight of the passionate edge—forever.

Still, once we decide to take this scary step toward the edge, leaving the old to embrace the new, we must bring some kind of closure to what we're leaving behind. If we don't, we often (1) fantasize about the past, as a result of too often choosing to live back there when the present becomes too difficult or doesn't turn out as we expected, or (2) condemn the past; looking back with contempt, we dismiss it, try to forget about it, and therefore lose out on everything it had to teach us.

The ultimate goal is to integrate the past into the present. Before we do that, we must learn when and how to say good-bye and how to internally process the "wasted years."

The Departure

When we consider leaving behind the sleepy years, it's important to ask ourselves the following questions: (1) Why do we so often fail to see the signs that it's time to depart? (2) How do we know when it's time to depart?

Why

We often fail to see the signs because we're afraid of losing something familiar. Think about it for a minute. What are you hanging onto? What are you afraid to let go of? What is holding you back from that next step toward the edge? It could be a job, a child, or a fear.

We often can't seem to leave one situation for another without feeling like a failure. To admit failure is horrible because it screams that we're inadequate, incompetent, or worth rejecting. No one will ever love us.

I head down this path quite frequently. It's a familiar path. So I stay where I am. "Bloom where you're planted," they say. This way you please everyone, don't shake up anyone's world, and everyone likes you. Good old Jean, or Dan, or Kelly—

▼

stable, solid and mature—boring, dull, and passionless. Those last three words scare me. We only get one life, right?

When boring, dull, and passionless are all we know, we have nothing to compare life to. When it fits warmly around us like a fur coat, what would ever make us want to cast it off?

Heat—only heat. Heat is what did it for me. Sometimes I have to almost suffocate, but if I get hot enough, I'll eventually do something.

How

How do we know when it's time to depart? This question is more difficult to answer.

The first sign for me is a restlessness, a stirring, a wondering feeling in my gut. I wonder if I'm supposed to be doing something different. I wonder if I'm supposed to be somewhere else. I wonder why I'm wondering about this. Then I usually start complaining about my distance from the edge. Then I pray. Then one day I know. Today's the day.

It might be different for you, especially if you're a more cautious person than I am. Once I decide, my feet become wings, and I fly for the edge just as fast as I can. I don't look back. I take little with me, and I tend to burn my bridges. I'm afraid if I don't, I might go back.

It has to do with change, something that threatens the most secure person.

I don't know. Maybe it's because I'm a child of the sixties, but stability threatens me more than change. Maybe I'm afraid if I stay in one spot, I'll die. Maybe I think that if I keep moving around, death (of any kind) won't catch me.

I have to admit that all of the moments leading up to the departure, plus the departure itself, are filled with anxiety, confusion, and often resentment that I'm even put in this awkward position in the first place.

As we're waking up, the crucial questions we must face about our present reality are: "So what *was* that the last ten (twenty, thirty, forty) years? Who was that? Was that me?"

Processing Those "Wasted" Years

When we finally wake up from those passionless years, it is a strong temptation to spend the next few years moaning around about how long it took us to wake up.

If we are truly committed to living on the passionate edge, we can't waste time wallowing in regrets. My wonderful friends patiently listened to me as I went on and on those first years I began to wake up: "I lost my entire twenties and half of my thirties. They're gone. I'll never get them back."

Whenever I took off on that tangent, it was a sure sign I was losing perspective, losing sight of eternity. I'm an eternal being, after all. Considering the fact that I'm going to live forever, I'm still just an infant at forty-two.

So, if it's unproductive to moan about those "wasted" years, what's productive?

Our hope lies in knowing three crucial truths about the past: (1) The past must be grieved—our part; (2) The past must be integrated into the present—our part; and (3) God is a Redeemer. He redeems each and every thing that we place in His hands—God's part.

Knowing and living out these three truths helps us understand that those passionless and seemingly often nonproductive years aren't wasted but are actually an extremely important part of our life journey.

Poor tormented and tortured Job, in the middle of his agony, cried out, "I know that my Redeemer lives" (Job 19:25). This was Job's hope, that his Lord would redeem. Before God could complete His part, redemption, Job had to fully enter into his part, the grief process.

The Stages of Grief

We have heard often about the stages of grief. I believe how each individual moves through these stages is determined by who the individual is and what or who is being grieved. For the sake of

▼

grieving our lost years, I'd like to look at the five stages: denial, repression, awareness, anger, and grief or acceptance. These are the ones I can identify in my own process.

Denial

Those who live far from the passionate edge are usually unconscious that this is what they're doing. There are, of course, others who we talked about in chapter four who, out of fear of risk or whatever, make the conscious choice to live without passion.

Most of us haven't a clue that there is such a thing as an incredibly full and passionate life and that we're missing it.

I can easily recall the years of denial—it's not difficult for me to touch those feelings once again. My days were filled with cleaning the kitchen, going back and forth to women's potlucks at church, and watching soap operas on television. No one ever probed, so I never thought much—about anything.

I remember asking a friend once, "Don't you ever get lonely?"

"Lonely?" she looked at me in surprise. "Lonely, well no, I don't think . . . well, I mean, I'm not sure. Well, no, not until . . . uh, yes, now that you mention it." She stared at me again, a look that said, "With friends like you, who needs enemies."

I asked another friend, "Do you get bored?"

"Bored?" Again, I received a surprised look.

"I do," I said. "I hate being bored."

She listened, as if this were all a brand new idea to her.

"For me, boredom is physically painful," I went on.

She looked suspicious. "What does it feel like?"

"It's a restlessness." I wiggled my shoulders. "You know, an uncomfortable feeling. It starts in my legs usually."

"Hmmm . . ." She thought for a moment. "Like in a meeting, do you ever want to jump up?"

We had several conversations after that on the subject, and if she'd ever been consciously aware of that restless feeling to be able to define it as boredom, she was now.

She was definitely in denial of her boredom. We joke about it now. She attributes her present feelings of boredom, at times, back to that first conversation.

You may wonder why awareness of our feelings of loneliness or boredom is necessary. What's wrong with some denial, a little less misery? Sorry, that's another book. There's always a reason for loneliness or boredom. For any feeling. We must always, whenever possible, honor our feelings. Find out where they come from and what they're telling us.

Awareness is always, in all circumstances, better than denial. It's only as we're aware, that we can possibly see God's working in a situation, and play a part in our growth.

Like my friends, some of us are brave enough once in a while to break out of denial. But it's so painful, even for a moment, to imagine where we could be in comparison with where we are and the work it takes to get there, that we immediately repress any feelings that surface. This repression can slap us right back into denial.

Repression

In my process, this stage varied from denial in one major way—in denial, for the most part, I was numb. In the repression stage, the feelings would begin to surface, but I'd immediately shove them back down. I knew that to give them any expression at all would be my undoing.

Simple questions would send me into Crazyland if I didn't repress them. Questions like:

"Where are you going on vacation this year?"

"Got any plans for New Year's Eve?"

"What are you doing this Sunday?"

Not that summer vacations, New Year's Eve, and Sundays have any special passion-invoking elements in themselves. But for me, part of the passionate life meant activity, any kind—enthusiasm, spontaneity, fun, adventure, going new places, meeting new people.

We never went on vacations—to spend money on a frivolous trip never even occurred to us. We went to bed by ten o'clock every night of the year. New Year's Eve was no exception. Sunday was church and nap day. We went to church in the morning and at night. We ate dinner. We took naps. We *never* varied the routine.

Those who are living now in the "wasted" years are repressing the seriousness, the magnitude, and the full intensity of their true feelings. Instead, they're saying things like: "Oh, I'm so tired. I really need a vacation." "Oh, (*husband's name*) just isn't very social. He's got a lot of great qualities. He's faithful and a good provider." "Oh, (*wife's name*) just doesn't seem that interested in sex anymore, but she's great with the children."

They may speak these words only to themselves. Or even say them to others, but deep inside, where their passions stir, the excuses don't wash. It's called "settling." These people become masters of deceit, sometimes even fooling themselves.

Awareness

Watch out for this stage because when the light begins to dawn, almost anything can happen, depending on the degree of passion we realize we've lost or how long we've been numb.

Awareness usually happens when we can't stand living away from the edge one more minute. It happens in one or both of the following two ways.

1. It becomes so dark away from the edge that we can't see at all. We start bumping into everyone and everything, causing injury and damage everywhere we go.

2. We suddenly catch a burst of light shining on those dancing along the edge, and that moment touches our passionate longing to be there.

Once I glimpsed the edge, there was no turning back. I had to be there. That was the point where I began to "throw off everything that hinders and the sin that so easily entangles" (Heb. 12:1). God has a race marked out for each of us. More than anything, I want to run this race with perseverance, my eyes fixed on Jesus, the Author and Perfector of my faith (Heb. 12:1–2). I can only do this fully aware, fully alive, fully ablaze with passion. Passion is what ignites our perseverance, our endurance, and our commitment to keep moving forward along the edge.

My decision to stay aware, of course, actually took place over many years. It's still taking place. I renew my commitment and vision regularly, sometimes as often as once a day or more when life gets especially hectic and/or tough. When awareness first hit me, however, something else tumbled in right on top of it.

Anger

I'm not sure with whom I was most angry at first. God? Those who had encouraged me in my position far from the edge? Myself?

We have plenty to be mad about. We feel betrayed. We're told: "Don't do that." "Don't say that." "Don't feel that." "Don't think that." "Don't want that." "Don't be like that." "Don't read that." "Don't listen to that." "Don't change that."

They want us to be safe, to be perfect, to be approved of—all in the name of love.

Who said safety, perfection, and/or approval was the goal?

The goal is to make something productive and useful out of the wasted years. We can only do that if we release the anger by fully expressing it.

It's difficult to find a safe place in which to express the anger. Sometimes our anger is of such an explosive nature, our loved ones run for cover. Who can blame them?

I found an objective support group during the period of my most intense anger. They didn't care what I said, how I said it, or how it came out.

I remember pounding my fist on the table one evening. "No one will ever rob me again!" I cried. Rob me? Of what? Of things like the opportunity to grow, my authentic self the way God created me, my feelings, my passionate pursuits, and my life.

It was only when I was able to express the anger that I could fully grieve the loss of those passionless years.

Grief or Acceptance

Underneath the anger is that sharp pain of loss. When we fully realize that we've lived in Numbsville for the last number of years and that those lost years can't be recovered—we can't go back and live them over again—a real sense of sadness enshrouds us.

It feels lousy, and we may try to shake it, but this stage may be the most important one because when we're at the end of this stage, we're at the end. If we can press through this grief, we can let go of the years and move on to finding passion in the future.

I recently watched one person who had just come through the anger stage and was beginning to enter the grief stage. We stood in the hall between our two offices.

"You can do this!" I cheered. "I'm proud of you. Keep going." I sounded exactly like my annoying morning work-out woman on television.

"Do I have to?" My friend looked at me soulfully, begging me to tell her there was another way. There had to be. This way was too hard. "Do I have to go through this?" Like a child throwing a tantrum, she banged her head against the wall.

True friend that I am, I nodded. "You have to, there's no other way." Truer words I'd never spoken.

She chose to go for it. I watched her grieve loss after loss. Now, a few months later, she's actually doing quite well. Just this week she told me about a passionate dream she'd had for many years, and how she planned to pursue it. She's already dreaming new dreams because she first grieved the lost years.

Integration

Integration is the time when we open up and let God redeem those numb years, making something meaningful out of them.

If we refuse to look at our past and give integration a good shot, we can't ever fully move on.

▼ What not to do with your past:
Deny it.
Repress it.
Fantasize it.
Scorn it.
Dishonor it.

▼ What to do with your past:
Embrace it.
Thank God for it.
Claim it.
Let God redeem it.
Integrate it.

Integrate is the word we want to focus on here. The other items on both lists are part of the integration process and will take care of themselves if we can learn to integrate our past into our present. Whether we believe it or not, we are a product of our pasts.

You can always tell how integrated a person is by how he talks about his past. If you hear bitterness toward certain people in that person's past who caused harm of any kind, that person is not yet integrated. A fully integrated person will speak of the past and the people in it with compassion, understanding, and forgiveness. Thinking or talking about it may still cause a degree of pain, but now the person has a perspective on the past. He has chosen not to let the past control the present, but he has chosen to integrate the past into the present, grow from it, and let it make him a better person.

To integrate something is to unify it, to make it whole. It is only as we integrate our past into the present that we can make some degree of sense of our lives and understand our true purpose in the passionate life that God intended for us to have.

For me, integration began the day I fully realized that God was a Redeemer. "I may be a product of my past, but I'm not a victim," I told myself. "There's something I can do here. I can take control." And I did, not overnight, but gradually. I began to look at the past in perspective and ask what it had to teach me now.

- ▼ My lonely childhood taught me about independence and creativity.
- ▼ My boyfriend's death in Vietnam taught me about life.
- ▼ My abusive marriage taught me about healing, forgiveness, and compassion.
- ▼ My divorce taught me about acceptance—of myself and others.
- ▼ My mother's death taught me about love.

If we bury the past as soon as it happens, like a buried treasure, it sits underground, precious and valuable but of no use until it's discovered and its value appreciated.

The past is full of buried treasure, passions, if you will, that once uncovered will make us rich beyond belief—in character, in growth, and in steps toward the passionate edge.

Don't be afraid. The deeper you dig, the more it may hurt, but it's only for a while. The joy of walking along the passionate edge far outweighs any pain of looking at the past.

God wants to redeem the past, but He can only do that if we let Him. In my experience, the number one obstacle we face in letting Him is the sudden explosion of pain in the core of our souls. Once we make the decision for integration, we decide for pain. We *invite* it in. Ouch.

———

S E V E N

▼

Passion and Pain

Pain hits us in degrees. Sometimes we wonder how we can handle one more difficult situation.

There are different kinds of pain. I distinctly remember several painful times in my life when I was five years old. First, I slammed the garage door on my finger so hard the whole nail ripped off. Second, my daddy died. I remember another time—after daddy died—I saw my mom kiss another man in the kitchen. Each of these incidents hurt; but the pain was different in each case.

I remember the time, also when I was five, when I caused someone else pain. A neighbor boy, Skip, handed me his BB gun and told me to shoot him. I did—right in the middle of his forehead. This time I had caused the pain.

As children, we needed help interpreting and processing events like these, but help may not have been available at the time. And so we are left to ourselves to try to make sense out of pain.

Unfortunately, pain is not something we think much about until we're in it, which means we usually have little control over it, and how it affects us and the others in our lives.

Just like me, you started learning about pain at a young age, too. Maybe you were sexually abused, or abandoned by a parent, or ridiculed by other children. Even if you just stubbed your toe, you learned something about pain.

Pain hurts. To combat the pain, we learn to do whatever it takes to survive, to stay out of pain, or to be happy. We learn to shut down our emotional selves. This is normal, especially in cases of abuse.

What we don't learn as children is that pain can lead to productive growth in our lives, and that shutting out pain is to shut out love, joy, friendship, wonder, growth, and so much more. It's to shut out passion, that encompasser of all emotions. How does this happen?

The First Shock

The first time we touch a hot stove, suffer a broken heart in our first love relationship, or lose our first loved one, we react with shock, anger, and confusion. We may react with thoughts like: *What just happened to me? How could this have happened to me? How dare this happen to me! I don't deserve this!*

That may or may not be true. Whether we deserved it or not didn't stop it from happening. The fact that we don't feel like we deserved it is significant; if we didn't deserve it, but it still happened anyway, we must not have a lot of control over the pain that can invade our lives at any given moment. With that knowledge comes a very real fear.

True passion encompasses the range of our emotional selves. Pain is one aspect, one part of the passion that comes with living on the edge. So pain in and of itself is not a hindrance to our pursuit of the passionate edge, but pain can hinder us and hold us back if we choose to internalize it instead of dealing with it by expressing it.

▼

In that first state of shock, though, we don't even know what's happening. All we know is that an unbearable suffering has invaded our bodies, our minds, and our souls. It feels sharp. It feels foreign. It feels awful.

You'd think that after living for thirty, fifty, or seventy years on the planet we'd be used to the hard stuff, we'd come to expect it and it wouldn't take us by surprise.

So why was I surprised when my twenty-one-year-old son announced he was moving to California? Doesn't everyone move to California at least once? I did when I was nineteen.

He was my firstborn. How could he leave me? There I went again—how could he leave *me? This isn't about me,* I reminded myself. Alone, never in front of him, I cried, screamed, and tried to face this. Finally, it was time for him to leave.

I remembered a six-year-old child going off to his first day of school with a little red lunchbox swinging at one side. We lived only a block from the school, and I ran over during recess. I clung to the fence, watching the children play, watching some older boys approach my son and push him over. I gasped, stealing myself not to climb the fence.

He got up, brushed himself off, and walked away. I trudged home, knowing I'd hear about it after school.

He came skipping in the door, full of news about his first day. He didn't even mention "the incident."

Now, at twenty-one, he loomed over me, and I was afraid they would knock him over once again.

"If they push you over . . ." I choked through my tears. "I . . ."

"If they push me over . . ." He was crying too. "I'm running home to my mom."

"I know you'll get up," I finished.

I was hurting, but this wasn't about me. My son was on his own journey.

"You'll get up," I repeated, believing it.

I had survived a first shock. What I felt now was great pride in my son who was also choosing the passionate edge.

Sometimes a first shock will cause me to cry out in pain to my children, "How can you do this to me?"

"I'm not doing this to you," they remind me patiently. "This isn't about you. It's about me."

This is always the truth. You see, first shocks throw us off balance, and we think it's all about us. When we're in pain, we think everything is about us.

All this time the thief is there, waiting to steal our passion, crying out, "Fool!" He's trying to make us believe it's all a cruel joke of God's—promising us abundant life and then giving us reality.

Are you ever tempted to fall for his line? How can we keep believing in the passionate edge if all it means is a life filled with torture and torment? Maybe it's not true, after all. Maybe we should join the millions of Americans, Christians among them, who grab a few videos and go into hibernation for the weekend—and many weeknights.

The hard part of this first stage of shock, maybe the hardest part, is that we feel ourselves shrinking away from the passionate edge. Who wants to sign up for pain? Of any kind? I'll be the first to admit that if there's another way, I'll take it.

There's never a way around, over, or under pain. I've tried them all. We must hang on. It's through the pain—or nothing. A daring adventure—or nothing. The passionate edge—or nothing.

Our hope lies in knowing that there is a way through pain. Pain is a vehicle. If we can just hang on, we can get to the other side—the passionate edge where there's joy.

Fear of Pain

I took my daughter to her group singing lesson this week. When it came time for the class members to get up individually and sing Karaoke in front of the class, one of the women began talking too fast, too much, and too loud. She was twitching in

▼

her chair and generally looking as if she might keel over from a cardiac attack at any minute.

When she stood up to sing, "aargh" was the first note we heard. Again and again she tried. "Aaargh" was all she could manage.

"When we're afraid," the instructor kindly began to explain, "our voice muscles contract. We can't get a clear, pure note. We can't express the true feeling the song evokes in us because fear is the overriding feeling. Fear tells our mind that we need to protect ourselves and all of our muscles contract to do that." He turned from the class to face her and said, "You can relax. You're among friends."

Fear never lets us walk along the passionate edge. Fear works overtime to protect us from our passion because passion involves pain, and pain hurts us. More clearly put, fear keeps us in a self-protective mode. When we allow self-protection to drive our lives, passion is nowhere to be found.

Now, even though the thief would like me to believe it's true, I'm no fool. I would never willingly invite pain into my life. If I had known that a life lived on the passionate edge included so much pain, I probably would be right out there with the rest of the folks—buying guns, saving every penny for my old age, and walking my children back and forth to school—protecting myself because something might happen to me, something bad.

I watched a number of senior citizens interviewed on television recently about why they chose to live in a certain senior citizen complex behind a large locked iron gate—like a fortress with guards all around.

"We're at a vulnerable age," one said.

"We need to protect ourselves," said another. "We're scared."

"Did we, the media, make you that way?" the reporter asked.

"Yes," they said.

The truth is, teenagers, not elderly people, are the most at risk when it comes to being potential victims of crime. Yet, these poor, elderly people are living out their lives in fear. They refuse to take risks of any kind. Something might hurt them.

Of course, then there's the elderly woman in our area who was recently attacked as she walked to her car late one evening. The attacker wanted her purse, but he got more than he bargained for. Being a hefty woman, she quickly overpowered him, got him on the ground, and began jumping up and down on his chest. Then she held him there until the police arrived.

When interviewed on the news, she simply said, "Well, he started it. He was trying to take my purse. I wasn't going to let him do that."

We may or may not agree with the aggressive way she handled the situation. The point is this woman is not driven by fear. She has learned something about living with passion.

Reality check:
We will face painful situations.
It's part of life on the passionate edge.

Question:
How badly do we want to live with passion?

———

We will never eliminate all moments of fear in our lives. That's not the goal, but God tells us, "Do not fear for I am with you" (Isa. 41:10). The goal is to stop and acknowledge Jesus' presence in the midst of fear.

We can't battle fear. It just grows bigger and bigger the more we try to fight it. The only thing we can do with our fear of pain is to choose to let it go.

Then take a giant step forward. Toward pain. Toward suffering. Toward the truth—that God wants abundant life for us—growth in passion.

Embracing the Pain

My first lesson in embracing pain occurred in an airport. My plane was moments from departing, and I couldn't tear myself away from two dear friends. The five days I'd spent in Colorado were a lesson in passionate growth like I'd not experienced in a long time. I was very much on the passionate edge and as a result, very much on the edge of pain.

I was quiet, wildly trying to suppress my feelings.

"What's up?" one of my friends asked.

"I don't want to leave." I could feel something breaking apart inside of me.

They put their arms around me. I started to cry—kind of, one tear. I tried to stop. I didn't want to feel this. My mother never cried.

"Embrace it," my friend coached.

"What?" I said.

"Head into it," the other one added.

"Embrace the pain. Let it happen. We're with you," they said.

Just like in my daughter's singing class, I was among friends.

Are you among friends? If so, let it happen. Head into it. Embrace your pain. It will change your life forever.

I wasn't used to embracing pain. I was used to running from it. Most of us run from it. I've only met a few people in my life who are so eager to walk on the passionate edge that they'll do anything—even suffer.

It took a few years for me to fully realize that without pain there is no passion. I thought my experience in the airport was a freak thing. I wasn't sure what I was supposed to learn, but I sure never thought the experience would repeat itself over and over again for the rest of my life every time I faced a choice—pain and passion or deadness.

The stages of shock and fear don't offer us a choice. As we've already seen, pain takes us by surprise sending us into shock. Right on the heels of the shock, sometimes even simultaneously, comes fear. It's then that we're faced with the awesome choice: "Do I run from this? Or do I embrace this?"

It's entirely up to you—every time you face pain of any kind. You should know that your decision will directly determine how much control the pain has over you, how productive the experience will turn out to be, and whether or not you live a life of passion.

Pain Management

Running from your pain puts pain in control, but choosing to embrace your pain is a decision to manage it; it puts you in control.

Clinical depression has controlled my fifteen-year-old daughter most of her life. Filled with unbearable pain, she has turned to unhealthy relationships with boys, acting out in anger, and a couple of suicide attempts. Somewhere along the line, she started to turn this huge, painful ship around.

Recently, we spent a few months away from each other. When we saw each other again, I asked, "So how are you feeling? Are you still depressed?"

She shrugged casually, "Oh, depression comes and goes, you know. I get lonely, I feel bad, but I know it won't be forever. I go for a walk, read a book, call a friend. It goes away."

Was this my daughter talking? The one who let depression drive her to attempt suicide only a short time before?

"God, You're awesome," I murmured.

At fifteen, so young, she was learning to manage her pain, something some adults never learn.

Jesus was the perfect role model for us. On the night of the last supper, He managed his pain when, knowing what Judas intended to do, He washed the betrayer's feet. He managed it again in the Garden of Gethsemane when, instead of running for the comfort of His Father, He stayed on His knees and let His soul and flesh fight it out, sweating drops of sweat and blood. He managed it as He hung on the cross. He could have sent for legions of angels but instead embraced His pain and chose death because it was God's will. What amazing strength.

So, managing our pain encompasses and assumes certain things: the freedom to choose, the will and desire to embrace rather than run, and the inner strength to suffer.

Choosing to embrace and manage pain rather than run from it isn't as easy as it may sound. Every time we fight a battle in our soul, I believe we build "spiritual muscles." We grow stronger every time we win.

This soul work is some of the hardest work you'll ever do in your life. That's what they tell women about having babies. "It's the hardest labor you'll ever have," they say.

We answer back, "Oh, sure. How hard can it be to push a baby out?"

We soon find out just how hard it is because we are birthing new life. Soul work, managing pain, is like that. We're birthing new life in our souls.

Heading into the Waves

The friends who told me, "Embrace your pain! Head into it!" made it sound so simple. "Head into it." I've never stood behind the wheel of any kind of boat, but I imagine you just turn the wheel and ride into the storm. Easy. Yeah, right.

On the one and only river rafting trip I took, our guide kept turning our raft toward the waves. It would be perfectly calm on one side of the river, and he'd head the raft toward the rough water on the other side.

"What are you doing?" I'd scream, knowing the answer full well. He was a maniac and trying to kill us.

Do you understand river rafting? You're *supposed* to head into the waves. That's the point. I never did get it.

Life. I still don't get it. I can't figure out why I always end up on the "wavy" side of the river. I'm moseying along, minding my own business, I think, and then bam, slam, crash! I'm up against waves on every side. I'm drenched. I'm fighting, slapping my oars as hard as I can against the waves, struggling to stay afloat. It's *supposed* to be that way.

On the river rafting trip, after each major wave, I'd grin at my rafting companions, hoping they'd noticed how valiantly I'd fought for my life. I'd made it. I'd fought the elements, and won. I was so proud of myself—the feeling of accomplishment, the sense of amazing courage, the skill—until the next wave. Then I'd get mad at our guide all over again, and the struggle to win against the waves would start again. That's what's *supposed* to happen.

I'm still doing that. I get mad every time the Guide heads our raft for the waves. The waves crash against, collide with, and roll over our raft. I become enraged. How dare this wave interrupt my life like this! My rage takes me through the wave. Sounds simple. It's not. It's so hard.

The poet Robert Bly says our country should have cried after Vietnam. We should have wailed, worn black, and grieved for our lost fathers, brothers, and sons. We didn't want to work that hard. The children of the sixties were just starting to grow up—buying BMWs, water skis, and condos; giving up on free love and getting married; drying out at detoxifying centers.

Grieving the forgotten in Vietnam never occurred to us. Those fathers, brothers, and sons who survived the war came home, and we all tried to pretend it never happened.

We, the people of America, have gotten a little bit sicker because of it. We buried a lot of pain and now we're paying for it—AIDS, violence, abuse. It has to come out somewhere.

It's no one's fault. It's everyone's fault. It's my fault. I don't always want to work hard at integrating my pain. It's like exercise. We will lose the weight. The muscles will one day be evident, but only if we're willing to sweat first.

Making Pain Productive

Many of us make it through our entire lives without ever heading into the waves. At the end of our lives, we pat ourselves on our backs and expect applause for making the trip without a wave touching us. The passionate edge is so far out of our reach, we couldn't touch it if we lived another seventy-five years.

Look at that elderly couple celebrating their fiftieth wedding anniversary. Bless their hearts. Someone throws a party. Everyone applauds. No one questions *how* they've spent their fifty years together. They may sit in front of the television every night, entertain their grandchildren every day, drive their motor home back and forth across the country. So what's wrong with that? They've earned it, after all. Fifty years!

Nothing's intrinsically wrong with that, but we must understand that longevity of years doesn't equal success on the passionate edge. It can mean just the opposite. Doing something for a long time, by its very nature, can equal death. Familiarity causes us to become numb to whatever it is we're doing.

The important issue is: what's going on inside? Inside the older man in front of the television? Inside the older woman playing with her grandchildren? Inside the individuals in the motor home?

Fifty years only equals success when internal growth is happening on the passionate edge. Too many of us stop on the edge of our pain long before we ever reach a fifty-year mark of any kind. Stopping on the edge of pain means stopping on the edge of growth.

Pain comes to all of us. We can't escape it. When it comes, we have a choice, remember. We can internalize it or embrace it. If we choose to internalize it, we can't make it productive. It eats us alive. We may go crazy at first, acting it out, but eventually we may end up like the older couple in the motor home—living lives of "quiet desperation"[1] as Henry David Thoreau so aptly put it.

Joe and Kelly Larson, friends of mine, were a "happily married" couple, or so everyone thought. Married for at least twenty years, they were raising three children, and had a home in the country, a dog, and everything—until Kelly realized how lonely she was. She longed to connect in a deeper way with Joe, but he was perfectly happy with the way things were. Instead, he tried to humor her. He sent her on spiritual retreats, paid for counseling, and supported everything she did in her discontent.

Instead of getting better, their relationship grew more strained because Kelly had begun to deal with the core of her pain. They fought more often because Kelly was no longer afraid of conflict. Finally, they heard the word neither of them thought they'd ever hear spoken in their home—*divorce.*

That word got Joe's attention. He loved Kelly. He didn't want to lose her. He didn't understand everything she was saying and he didn't know if he could give her everything she was asking for, but he had to try.

On his own, he called a therapist and began his own counseling. In these sessions, all kinds of unresolved childhood issues were uncovered that had caused him to emotionally distance himself from Kelly. He began to face these issues and slowly, gradually, he turned his pain into growth.

Now, several years later, with no prodding from Kelly, Joe goes on his own spiritual retreats. They communicate in a way they never have before—emotionally and spiritually. They are committed to growth as a couple and individually.

Like Joe and Kelly, we must *commit* ourselves to the journey. It's the *only* way to the passionate edge. We must learn how to turn our pain into productive growth and no matter how big the waves get, we must stay in the raft.

A Deeper Passion

Pain doesn't scare me anymore. It still hurts, but it doesn't scare me. Now I know what to do with it.

We're only scared of what we don't understand or can't control. Life on the passionate edge empowers. Because I've made the choice to stay in the raft and head into the waves, pain can't destroy me. I've chosen it. Because I've chosen it, I have the privilege of using it for good and for God and his eternal purpose in my life.

Pain deepens our passion and actually makes life on the edge a more enriching experience. Because we've known darkness, colors are brighter. Because we've known discord, harmony is sweeter. Because we've known evil, righteousness is purer.

91

▼

Embracing pain brings the passionate edge closer than anything else we might do. We can't reduce this process to a formula. No matter how often we sit in a class on swimming and listen to the instructor ramble on about how to swim, we don't learn how to swim until we dive into the water. If we don't want to sink, we swim.

A friend of mine told me after I quit my last job, "Gloria, I haven't had one feeling since you've been gone."

I smiled. I knew exactly what she meant. I was the person in her life that she depended on to ask her about her feelings, to "keep her on the edge." Without feeling her feelings, she feared she may have stopped growing.

Talking about our feelings helps us stay in touch with them, feel them fully, and work them through. If I could offer only one how-to on the subject of pain on the passionate edge, I offer two words: Feel it.

Sounds simple? I dare you to feel, really feel, every wave, every pain you collide with in a week or in a day. God gives us that kind of courage. Pull it up.

EIGHT

▼

CHASING THE WIND

If I could ask God just one question, I'd ask, "What's the meaning of life?" That's the first question I'll ask Him when I get to heaven, but I really wonder if I can wait that long for the answer.

Sometimes I think the answer is about faith. Other times I think it's about redemption. Then sometimes it seems as simple as survival, which is ridiculous. Why would God put us here just to watch us flail and kick around for a few years—to see how long we can all live together without totally annihilating one another? That doesn't sound like God. That sounds like me when I was little playing army in the dirt with the neighbor boys.

My friend Jan never even thinks about the meaning of life. How can she not even think about it? I think about it at least once a day, usually more. Often I obsess on it, trying to figure it out so I'm sure I'm with the program. I don't want to miss anything. I don't want to find out some day that meaning was happening somewhere down here and I missed it.

▼

A few verses in Ecclesiastes have always bothered me. You know the ones:

> "Meaningless! Meaningless!" says the Teacher. "Utterly meaningless! Everything is meaningless."
>
> Is there anything of which one can say, "Look! This is something new"? It was here already, long ago; it was here before our time. . . .
>
> I have seen all the things that are done under the sun; all of them are meaningless, a chasing after the wind.
>
> Ecclesiastes 1:2, 10, 14

So what does all of this mean? Who wants to chase after the wind? Why try to find meaning if it can't be found? Why in the world approach the passionate edge if we can't expect to find meaning once we're there?

It's a cycle we keep falling into. Like the spin cycle on our washing machine, we're wrung out when the machine finally bumps to a stop. Without passion to drive us, we can't find meaning. Without meaning, why pursue passion? Is it really all a chasing after the wind?

Meaningless Endeavors

Do you think about the meaning of life? I've been told more than once that I ask "disturbing" questions. So, someone has to do it.

The writer of Ecclesiastes asked a disturbing question: "Is there anything of which one can say, 'Look! This is something new'?" (Eccles. 1:10). I think that's pretty disturbing.

If, since the beginning of time, we're just doing the same stuff over and over, functioning as muffled echoes of each other down through time, what good is that?

What exactly is a meaningless endeavor and how does it hinder us in our pursuit of the passionate edge? In some ways, I suppose, meaningless endeavors are all relative. My meaningless endeavor might have significance to you and vice versa. For me, a meaningless endeavor might be a dumb conversation at a shower, makeup party, or church. I have dumb conversations at these places all the time, often with complete strangers. For you, a meaningless endeavor might be breaking your leg playing volleyball.

Maybe it's a matter of perspective. My friend, Jan, the one who never thinks about the meaning of life, has dumb conversations at the above places, too, but she sees these conversations as necessary encounters on the way to potential relationships down the road, possibly meaningful friendships. Maybe I should hang around Jan. I'd have necessary encounters rather than meaningless endeavors.

Actually, the above kind of meaningless endeavor may not affect your pursuit of passion as much as the kind that distracts, detours, disillusions, or derails you.

The Distraction

This can be anything from a new computer to an obsession with golf, bridge, or food (mine). I have some friends who are distracted by *ministry*. While once a meaningful passion, their ministry has become simply a meaningless distraction, something to fill their time and give them a false sense of self-importance.

You know you're distracted when you're going through the motion of putting one foot in front of the other, but the bounce has long since gone out of your step.

The Detour

This kind of meaninglessness can take a seemingly positive form: a new relationship, a new job, or a new hot tub. It may feel like we're on track because this new thing feels satisfying and fulfilling to us, but even good things can consume us and take us on a detour that can soon become meaningless.

I recently wrote a mission statement for my life. It reads:

To compassionately wipe away the tears of pain and sorrow, to gently bring a smile to faces everywhere, to courageously bring healing to the people of my world, to grow in God's intended authenticity and to passionately love God, and in all integrity, communicate to others God's love and redemptive purposes through the use of my pencil, my ears, my mouth, my hands, and my heart.

I also wrote a mission statement for specific areas of my life such as writing and parenting.

Whenever an activity or relationship begins to take me away from my mission, it's a detour. I must recognize it and make the necessary adjustment.

The Disillusionment

Everything feels meaningless when we're in a state of disillusionment or disappointment. No matter what we do, it makes no sense. Nothing matters. We don't care. The passionate edge drifts further away and we watch it go, unable to muster up enough feeling to even care that it's almost out of sight.

The meaningless endeavor of disillusionment comes in many forms: a child who won't heal, a marriage that won't mend, or a God who seems distant. We can't make sense of any of it. I've been there. I have no plans to return.

The Derailment

I derailed once a few years ago. Of course, at that time, I didn't know there was a passionate edge, a place to walk that was exciting, adventuresome, creative—passionate. I was simply plodding, putting one foot in front of the other—each step sinking a little deeper into a self-centered, self-protective, and self-motivated sludge. Being in a derailed state means every day is filled with taking care of oneself so that life's pain doesn't take over.

It's often a matter of perspective. It was certainly not in "my plan" to become a single parent of five children. At the time, it felt like a meaningless derailment.

Now I know that it's largely because of becoming a single parent, because of the derailment, that I discovered the passionate edge in the first place. Sometimes the sludge has to get really deep before we start digging our way out. But when we do, we find direction, purpose, and meaning. It begins with an understanding of who's responsible.

Who's Responsible?

When I feel caught in the throes of a meaningless endeavor, I immediately blame whoever or whatever I think is causing the meaninglessness and making my life less than passionate and adventuresome.

I get bored easily.

"I'm moving to Hawaii," I told a friend recently. I could already see the aqua blue ocean and feel the warm island breeze on my cheeks and the fine white sand between my toes.

"Why?" She looked shocked.

No wonder she was asking. I'd recently moved to an apartment in a Seattle suburb and had seemed quite happy.

"Oh," I searched for a reason. "Seattle's gotten so violent lately. It rains too much here. I'm tired of the traffic. It's a drag, you know." The more I talked, the more I realized I was touching feelings I wasn't sure I wanted to touch. "Nothing's happening here. And you never want to do anything different." Oh, now I was attacking my friend, depending on her to entertain me.

She looked hurt, understandably. I kept whining until she got mad.

"It's not my fault you're bored," she said. "And it's not Seattle's fault either."

"It's my job," I said.

"No, it's not. It's you. A new job, a new city, a new friend—none of these things can keep you constantly stimulated. Get a life," she said.

Nice friend. The kind who tells you the truth.

Before I could get packed and move to Hawaii, I had the opportunity to accompany a ministry team into a state prison.

For some reason I felt more at home there than anywhere I'd been in a long time. The inmates loved us, and we loved them.

I saw an opportunity for meaningful activity, and I plan to make "the most of every opportunity" (Eph. 5:16). Soon, going into prison and sharing spiritual insights with the inmates will be a regular part of my life. I can't wait.

Much to my friend's relief (after she got over being mad, she confessed she'd miss me if I moved), I haven't talked about Hawaii since that day.

The moral of this embarrassing story is that if we're experiencing meaninglessness in our lives, I'm afraid we're the ones responsible. Actually, that's good news. We can often change what we know we're responsible for.

Being the one responsible doesn't mean that changing jobs, cities, or friends isn't necessary. Often it is. In my case getting restless and feeling like I'm always just chasing after the wind tends to be a pattern. My frank friend, who knows me so well, confronts this pattern and, in doing so, makes me face reality.

If we refuse to take responsibility for the meaninglessness in our lives, we become victims of that meaninglessness, always blaming someone and something outside of ourselves, waiting for an external someone or an external something to give our lives direction, meaning, and purpose—a significant person of the opposite sex, challenging job, or material object.

It's up to us to discover passionate meaning in our lives' activities. Fortunately, we're not alone on this journey. While meaning comes from within ourselves, it takes Someone else to help us discover it.

Your Silent Partner

I believe that knowing God and staying on a passionate spiritual journey is the only way to find meaning in anything we do and in the becoming of who we are. Knowing God connects us with eternity and our eternal calling.

Sometimes I have a hard time separating myself from my various roles—mother, writer, friend. If God has called me to be something, like a mother for example, then that's who I am, even if being involves doing. In being that, I find eternal meaning.

I don't know about you, but I can only find meaning in what stirs my passion. Passion in this sense doesn't necessarily mean happy, wonderful feelings. Finding meaning as a mom of five teenagers at the moment doesn't mean that I jump out of bed each morning thrilled to tackle one more discussion about grades, clothes, or curfew.

What it does mean is that I'm able to step back from a situation that may momentarily feel meaningless and allow God to show me the purpose, how I can turn it into something productive that will keep me on the passionate edge.

For example, as children do, a number of times, my children have gotten into altercations with other children. I, as the person who wants to find passionate meaning in everything, view each altercation as the opportunity to teach my children how to love their world.

For example: "I hate Tiffany!" Merilee runs into the house, screaming. "She . . . [blah, blah, blah]." She then reports the latest thing Tiffany did.

"Oh, no, that's terrible," I cry, grabbing my daughter by the hand, ready to march over to Tiffany's and settle the matter. But before I can even slip on my shoes, inevitably the phone rings and Tiffany informs my daughter that she can't play with her for two weeks or five months or whatever Tiffany's mother figures is punishment enough for the specific crime.

As it turns out, each time my daughter is as guilty as Tiffany, but Tiffany's mother never gives any of us the opportunity to find meaning in the conflict. Her answer is always to separate the girls.

It's frustrating, and I've cried out to my Silent Partner more times than I can count. "What now, God? This feels totally nonproductive. What good is all of this unresolved conflict?" I ask.

I have the uncomfortable feeling that Tiffany's mom refuses to resolve conflict with her husband and her own children also. It's too bad.

Sometimes I can't find immediate meaning, but over the years as I've watched parents react to their children's various squabbles, my children and I have learned a lot about conflict resolution and how working through conflict can make better people out of everyone. I have never taught my children to run from conflict, and I've learned that whether or not the other parties wish to be involved, God will help us discover meaning in the hard places.

I call God the Silent Partner in this because the process of turning meaningless endeavors into passionate pursuits of meaning is often a quiet work of the soul. God waits for us to quit flailing, to stand back, and to invite Him and His wisdom into the process. Then, ever so quietly, He goes about helping us make sense of the various aspects of the situation so that we can grow in our passion.

One question I often hear people asking and one I myself ask a lot is, just how involved does God want to be? According to Jeremiah 29:11, He wants to be very involved: "'For I know the plans I have for you,' declares the LORD, 'plans to prosper you and not to harm you, plans to give you hope and a future.'"

The Plan

Hope and a future—I take this to mean that no matter what the situation, God has a plan for meaning. For every painful circumstance, for every crazy act of violence, for every seemingly meaningless endeavor.

That's God's part. He gives us hope and a future. Our part is to plug into the plan. God's plan to turn meaningless endeavors into meaningful events looks something like this:

▼

Meaningless endeavor + pain and/or wasted time + integration = passionate significance.

———

Meaningless endeavors take us off the track and keep us from the passionate edge *only* when we can't find a way to turn them into something meaningful. I believe, if we're looking hard enough, we can find meaning in the most mundane and senseless situations.

We couldn't imagine why the war in Vietnam went on and on and on. Senseless killing? Only if that's how you choose to view it.

Why wasn't my friend's seventeen-year-old daughter healed of that brain tumor? What could the purpose possibly be? Of course, at a time like that, who even cares about the purpose? We'd rather have the person.

What kind of meaning could possibly come out of the humiliation and pain caused my two sons the night they were arrested just because they happened to accompany someone who, unbeknownst to them, committed a petty theft?

Who even cares about meaning and purpose when you're in so much pain? If we're going to live on the passionate edge, we have to care. We have to care a lot. We have to make as much sense out of it as we can so that we can continue to move forward.

God does everything in His power to make us stop and look, really look, at the event, situation, circumstance, or whatever it is. He wants us to feel its impact. Since this usually involves pain, as we've already seen in the last chapter, this is often where we bow out—we reach for the remote to change the channel. Why would we want to deliberately and consciously sign up for pain?

If we can make it to integration, we can move through to passionate significance.

When we first become aware of the passionate edge, we don't have a clue as to how to get there, let alone walk there, or dance there. We don't care about meaning. All we want is relief from the painful growth.

▼

Somewhere along the line we become aware of the bigger picture, the overall plan. This isn't just about us in pain. This is about courage, love, and redemption. This is about resisting the thief and grasping the abundant life that Jesus promised. This is about drawing close to the passionate edge.

We don't know what that looks like when we first start out, but early into the journey we begin to get an inkling that we're in for the most daring adventure of our lives because God has a plan. His plan for me looks different than His plan for you.

I used to think that following the step, "God has a wonderful plan for your life," in the "Four Spiritual Laws" tract was easily enough applied. That simply meant that I would get married to a wonderful man, have a number of wonderful children, live in a wonderful house, attend a wonderful church, and have a wonderful life happily ever after. No, God's plan is a bit more complex than that.

Passionate Redeemer

I talk a lot in this book about God as Redeemer because if we're ever going to move toward the passionate edge and dance along it, we must understand God's involvement in our lives, how it doesn't matter *that* we survive whatever the situation is, but *how* we choose to survive, *how* much we allow God to be involved, and *how* much we resist or cooperate.

One thing I love about the passionate life is that it's a life of redemption. There is always, always, always hope.

Almost two years ago, I started through a period with my then-thirteen-year-old daughter that felt thoroughly meaningless. Nothing felt productive. No matter what I did, it seemed to turn out wrong.

I tried strict discipline. "You're in your room with the door shut for a week."

I tried counseling. "This mother doesn't understand normal puberty," the counselor wrote on our form, I found out later. My daughter got kicked out of school eight times in two months, entertained herself by going to the mall and taking whatever she felt like without paying for it, ran away for days at a time, was verbally and emotionally abusing me and her younger sister, and was suicidal. This was normal puberty?

I tried medication.

"Prozac, the new miracle drug, will do it."

I tried ignoring her.

"You don't care about me. I knew it all along."

Finally two years later, I'm seeing the redemption. I'm exhausted, but it's finally happening. All of that seemingly futile effort is starting to mean something.

The one thing I did right was refuse to abandon my daughter. That one thing has communicated love to her. Along the way I got frustrated, but we talked. I blew up, but I took responsibility and repented. I left, but I always came back. Now I'm watching God redeem every lousy action, every damaging statement, and every emotional accusation.

At the moment, she's fifteen and pregnant. On a support group form, she had to answer two questions: Who in your life do you admire the most, and who in your life has supported you the most in this pregnancy? Her answers to both questions were the same: "My mom."

That has to be God's redemption at work. It has to be. After all we went through, there is no reason any of this should work out for us. There was something at work trying to destroy our relationship, but because of God's redemptive power, we're finding meaning.

Why let meaningless endeavors keep us from the passionate edge when God is available to redeem them?

———

NINE

▼

IGNITING THE SPARK

Mom, how could it be that God doesn't have a beginning and an end?"

"Mom, why doesn't the devil like God?"

"Hey, Mom, how come God made all the bad people?"

These are only a few of the "theological" questions I asked my mother as I was growing up. We had many theological discussions. We didn't often arrive at conclusions, but we enjoyed asking the questions and kicking around the possible answers. She never stopped our exploratory discussions with "the Bible says," because my mom didn't really know what the Bible said. The Bible was kind of a decoration in our home.

I have prayed ever since I could talk. Some of my first words as a small child were, "Now I lay me down to sleep. . . . " It's like I was born with a passion for God and a mind that thrived on exploring spiritual questions.

However, at the age of nineteen, I entered a "religious" cult-like atmosphere where I was told what to believe almost every minute of every day—no more questions, no more spiritual ponderings, no more wondering about anything spiritual.

The answers were suddenly clear cut for me, right there for me in black and white in the Bible. That's what they all told me—black and white principles in black and white print. All I had to do was read it. If I didn't understand it, if it didn't seem black and white to me, all I had to do was say so and they would explain it. They told me the spiritually enlightened understood these things. Some day I hoped to be one of these "spiritually enlightened." I wanted to "get it" the way they did.

I never got it. What I did get was a lot of spiritual abuse:

"If you sin, you'll go to hell. Just like that. So you better not die in sin."

"The Bible says, 'If you love me, you'll keep my commandments.' You just sinned, so obviously you don't love God."

"You can't wear that mini-skirt to church. You wouldn't even want to unless you have the heart of a Jezebel."

What was the heart of a Jezebel? I wasn't sure, but I knew it wasn't a compliment.

I don't know exactly when it was that I started dying, falling asleep, or whatever you want to call it. All I know was that it seemed God was mad at me all the time because I was always doing something to set Him off. In my mind, the only way to live the perfect Christian life was to die to any kind of passion that might cause me to sin or take me over the edge. This wasn't a conscious decision, but it's what I let happen.

We may shut down our spiritual passion for any number of reasons. What we don't realize, because it's on an unconscious level, is that when we shut down our passion for fear of sinning or for any other reason, we shut down all over. Without passion, nothing is alive—not our souls, not our emotions, not our spirits.

Oh, we can still shout and sing, and often do, sometimes in church. But it's not coming from the inside; without passion, it can't. What happens is that we're simply stirred from the outside by external stimuli.

So? So, it's not real. We're just going through the motions. We often hear people say, "I'm just not excited about church, the Bible, or prayer like I used to be." So they try a new church, attend a new Bible study, or join a new prayer group. None of these things will help if their spiritual passion has died. The flame must be reignited. They must reconnect with God.

Reconnecting with God

A new connection or a new relationship starts with a question. Who are you, really? The deepest relationships and the closest of friendships have this question at their core, and it is asked again and again, sometimes every day.

The relationship grows as both individuals get answers to that question a little at a time, until they can honestly say that they *know* one another. Even then they must keep asking the question because people are always changing. Who I am today is different than who I will be tomorrow, and knowing you today is different in many ways than knowing you tomorrow.

God never changes. We must keep asking who He is though. He is so big. If we lived a thousand lifetimes, we'd never discover all there is to know about Him.

He is our Creator and the One who gives us life to begin with. It only makes sense that when we let that life die, He is the only One who can bring it back—if we cooperate by continuing to ask the above question.

One reason our passion dies in the first place is because we and those who have gone before us think we know all there is to know about God. We read the Bible and figure if we memorize as much Scripture as possible, we'll never have to do anything else.

It's not quite that simple. We're human beings and fallible. We'll never rationally explain the glorious mysteries of the God who loves us supremely.

106

▼

What I do know is that a heart turned toward God is one that eventually connects with Him. Even in my disconnected state, God searched for ways to connect. Finally, when I was able to admit that I knew nothing about Him, He began to illuminate Himself, and I began to know Him in a way I never had. I decided no one would ever again stop me from asking Him, "Who are You, really?" I would ask, and I would discover for myself. "If you seek him, he will be found by you" (1 Chron. 28:9b).

"Who are You?"

I felt God's presence as I walked alone out of the Grand Canyon.

"Who are You?"

"For God so loved the world, that He gave His only begotten Son, that whosoever believeth in Him should not perish, but have everlasting life" (John 3:16, KJV).

"Who are You?"

I saw God in my teenage daughter, of all places.

Why, He was everywhere. He always was everywhere. I'd just missed Him because I wasn't awake. Now that I'd discovered the passionate edge, God appeared at regular intervals.

If I was listening, He'd talk. If I was watching, He'd move. If I was awake, He'd do something far greater than I dared to dream.

This doesn't mean we can't learn who God is from other people. When we're truly alive, we learn who He is from everyone and every situation we encounter. Your spiritual journey is different than mine, and God meets you in places and ways that He'd never meet me—guaranteed.

"Who are you?" is a question we must ask every day and never quit asking.

Reevaluating Our Spiritual Journey

Asking God "Who are You, really?" is only the first, but probably most important, step we take toward Him when our passion begins to waken. Reconnecting with God leads to an entire reevaluation of our spiritual journey.

It's truly one of the most frightening moments in life—at least it was for me—to think we have all of the answers and then suddenly one day to realize we barely know the questions. It's akin to a confident dive off the high board, remembering halfway down we can't swim.

Now what?

Again, the walk on the passionate edge, the reevaluation of our spiritual journey, starts with questions, not answers. Secretly in my mind, because I couldn't ask the questions out loud, I began to wonder about life and death, "accidents," good and evil, destiny, and heaven and hell. I began to wonder if everything I was taught by pastors, everything I'd read in Christian books, and everything I'd learned from other "saints" was really the truth.

Just for the record, those in the reevaluation process are really not trying to be irreverent when "strange" questions pop into their minds and they speak them out loud—well, not most of the time. When I first started reevaluating my spiritual journey, many of the people around me seemed slightly amused by my questions. They placated me by pretending to have a conversation and to wonder and wander down the philosophical road as long as they could stand it. Then, of course, these folks would have to arrive at some conclusion, weak though it was, about the subject.

These conclusions made me uncomfortable. How could we *know* beyond any doubt that God did or was—anything? Wouldn't we have to be God then? As finite, sinful human beings, how could we aspire to know anything?

Because everyone seemed to know the answers, I became more uncomfortable with every conclusive conversation and more comfortable with my questions.

I know some things. I know that God is the Creator and that He's all-powerful, all-knowing, and ever-present. I know He's absolutely, wonderfully, incredibly, and overwhelmingly good and full of grace, mercy, and truth. I believe with all my heart that Jesus Christ died on the cross for my sins.

Beyond this, I don't know much. I don't know where the heathens in Africa who have never heard about Jesus spend eternity. I don't know why "Christians" die in car accidents, with brain tumors, and of AIDS, or why anyone else does.

When 132 people died in a plane crash in Pennsylvania, I didn't know why. I don't know why I get on a plane at least ten times each year and my plane stays in the air—so far. I don't know why any of these things are the way they are.

I think what's important is that since beginning a reevaluation of my spiritual journey on the passionate edge, I no longer need to know. "Why" doesn't matter like it once did. I'm learning to trust God with the answers.

You know the old saying, "Love means never having to say you're sorry." I'd like to offer this to those awakening to passion: "Passion means never having to ask why." Passion on the spiritual journey means living for God as hard as we can—without knowing the whys. That's not only passion; that's faith.

Everyone, my friends and family, patted me on the head when I first started asking "disturbing" questions out loud. They thought it was a phase or it would pass. It hasn't. I believe, as much as I've ever believed anything, that reevaluating the spiritual journey on the passionate edge is a daily endeavor. We must keep doing it, even if it means driving everyone crazy in the process.

The Bible tells us to "fan into flame the gift of God" (2 Tim. 1:6). One of the benefits of the continual reevaluating of our spiritual lives is that it fans our gifts into flame.

Fanning the Gift into Flame

When we're asleep our gifts lie dormant, or maybe I should say the effectiveness of our gifts for the kingdom of God is debatable. I do see zombie-type passionless folks using their gifts, and I see other people respond—like the Balaam's ass story found

▼

in Numbers 22. If a person is a true searcher, God will use whatever is handy to reach that person.

If we want to participate in God's plan of redemption, and I do, then we have to touch our passions so that our gifts can come to life and, in turn, move others to life.

I believe God gives us gifts at birth—or maybe even before conception. He deposits gifts deep into our personalities, gifts He wants us to use for good in His kingdom. It's up to us to let our passion fan these gifts into flame—surface them, identify them, and put them into motion. Cooperate with God in bringing them to life.

In Jesus' parable of the talents (Matt. 25:14–30), the servant who buried his one talent was thrown into outer darkness by his master. I'm not sure what this means, but I do wonder if it means that those of us who fail to bring our talents to life and use them will miss out on the victory party.

The Bible says the servant buried his talent because he was afraid. That enemy of our souls strikes again—fear. In the struggle to stay alive on the passionate edge, we will do continual battle with fear.

Jesus didn't explain this parable; He told the story and left the interpretation up to us. If the master was truly a hard man as the servant claimed, harvesting where he hadn't sown and gathering where he hadn't scattered seed, then can we really blame the servant for being afraid? It would mean he would have to be "instant in season and out of season" (2 Tim. 4:2), always prepared in case the master wanted him to use his talent. It would be so easy to fail. Wouldn't the best thing be to bury the talent, hang on to it, and keep it safe?

It makes the master look not only hard but a little disorganized, like he doesn't have a plan and does what he feels like doing when he feels like doing it. Spontaneous, passionate, and each moment bursting with—God.

What kind of way is that to live? It's truly life on the passionate edge—full of surprises, unplanned detours, unexplained spiritual revelations of redemption, wonderings, and ponderings that don't go anywhere that we know of, starts without finishes—that we can see, questions and more questions (the answers of which remain hidden to us, because there are none).

When we become alive to our spiritual gifts we can't worry about things like failure, getting it right, or what people think. When passion ignites our gifts, we explode onto the scene, focused on only dancing along the edge and using our gifts that others might take notice—not of us, but of God—and want to join us.

We humans given to distraction can only focus when we're trusting that God is the One watching out for our passion and that between the two of us our soul is being cared for.

Caring for Your Soul

Until recently, I never considered that my soul needed tending to. In his book, *Care of the Soul,* Thomas Moore convinced me that this is important, not only important but crucial.

I always thought it was called living the Christian life. You know the big three: read the Bible, listen to the sermon on Sunday morning, and pray.

When nothing happened anymore, even though I was doing all those things as always, I knew I was ready for something else, another step.

Passion nurtures and constantly feeds, drives, and motivates. I have never met a person who, once beginning the passionate journey, didn't realize that a huge part of that journey meant spiritual growth and nurture of the soul.

We care for our souls when we take a nature walk, when we stop in the middle of a busy day and whisper, "God," or when we light a candle and celebrate who Jesus said He is (the light of the world).

We care for our soul anytime we remember that we are eternal beings. Our lives are about more than going to school or work, entertaining friends, getting married and raising children, playing sports, and "finding ourselves."

Our lives are about passionate growth of the soul and spirit as it relates to God and others. Of course, the journey may include all of the above, but when we begin to focus on any of that temporal stuff, we're way off center.

As we've already seen, it's not about viewing our lives through the "why" lens of a cosmic camera, asking why things happen so that we have understanding, comfort, and/or peace, and therefore less suffering.

No, it's viewing our lives through the "hmmm" lens. We ponder, we wonder, and we pray so that we might become. That's what God cares about—who we become as we live our lives.

Yesterday my child was caught doing something bad. It broke my heart, which often happens to parents of children who sometimes do bad things.

I cried out to God, "I don't care what the parenting books say. I don't care what the talk shows say. I don't even care what the other parents in my church would do with their teens under these circumstances. All I care about, God, is what You say. What are You saying?"

For a change, I recognized a soul-making opportunity. How could my child and I care for our souls in this situation? Who could we become through this? This is what I talked to my child about. Not "Oh, God, why did this happen to us?" It doesn't matter why it happened. No, what matters is, "Who can we become?"

As we progressed through this particular soul-making event, we became different people, she a little more sober and wiser and I a bit more compassionate and humble.

If we can learn to care for our souls, our motivation for the spiritual journey will be based on a love relationship with God because we'll understand that we're in this together. We do and are nothing outside of Him.

Loving God

How can you passionately love someone in a relationship that's based on faith alone? How do you communicate when you can't see, hear, smell, taste, or touch the other party? How?

I know we can't *make* it happen. My son went to a "rave" (an underground dance and drug party that takes place in a warehouse and lasts all night long) last week and had a spiritual experience, the kind I never could have orchestrated for him, no matter how much I manipulated or coerced. God met him where he was—at a *rave*. I've prayed for him for years, wrung my hands with each of his new "trips," fretted, and worried that he would never wake up to the spiritual journey. Why now? Why at a rave? Why not in a more traditional way? God only knows.

For me, I'm more passionately in love with God than I have been since as a child I first acknowledged His presence in my life. Why now? Because I'm finally asking God who He is, and this is what I'm encouraging my son to do, whether he's at a rave or a church service.

This passion I feel for God has shown me what also can happen between couples and even friends. You can't really passionately love someone unless you really passionately know someone. Knowing someone takes time—years.

Knowing God happens when we awaken and begin to move toward the passionate edge and reconnect with Him. It happens along the way as we reevaluate our spiritual journey. It happens as we fan our gifts into flame and learn how to let God use them for good. It happens as we care for our souls.

How can you not fall passionately in love with someone who died for you? Who loves you with everything in His being? Who is full of grace, mercy, and truth? Who is all good? Who keeps loving you again and again and again—no matter what you do or who you are? You don't have to try to fall passionately in love with God. If you know Him and live on the passionate edge, you can't *help* it.

TEN

▼

THE BOUNDARIES
OF FREEDOM

How can we really appreciate our legs unless we've spent time in a wheelchair? Doesn't affluence mean more to someone who's lived a good portion of his or her life in the slums? I suppose we can only truly appreciate the feeling of walking free along the beach if we've spent time behind the cold steel bars of a prison.

There was a poignant moment during one of my visits to the women's prison this year that I'll never forget. One of the women touched my earrings and said, "Oh, are hoops back in again?" She would never know. She was in for life. Another woman asked about my children. Her four were spread all over the country at various relatives' homes and would continue to be there for a long, long time.

Someone may think, *Well, if they're in prison, it's their own fault.* It's easy to look at the situation on the surface and make a quick judgment. If we think about it, we know there has to be more to any situation than what we see on the surface. It's not quite that simple. Besides, the point is not whose fault anything is. So what *is* the point? Someone's gone over the edge. Because of her own mistakes or because she was a victim of someone else, a life has gone over the edge.

Jesus, fortunately, didn't die only for those who keep themselves pure all of their lives. He died for those of us who went over the edge, many of us more than once. He's in the business not of patting perfect people on the head but of redeeming sinners. That's why the "perfect" people—the Pharisees—tend to get a little upset with the rest of us, and you really can't blame them. Jesus pays too much attention to us sinners.

I, for one, am grateful. No, I'm not proud of being a sinner, but the only reason I've ever been able to recover from my going-over-the-edge times is because of Christ's redemption. Like some of those women in prison, I may deserve a life sentence, but because of His mercy and redemption I didn't receive a life sentence. I got freedom and another chance, and another, and another, ad infinitum.

I've often wished I understood the gift of freedom before I received the gift of passion. I might not have tumbled over the edge as often and as far as I did. Passion and freedom go hand in hand. To abuse one is to abuse the other.

Passionate Freedom

The nature of freedom implies the privilege of making choices. Those of us who have become victims of abusive people know that the first thing we lose is our freedom to choose. The only choice we have is to "obey" our abuser. Of course, it doesn't take an abusive situation to put a person in prison. We can imprison ourselves to our own rigid set of rules, too. We can take away our own freedom.

Unlike trust and respect, freedom is not something we earn in the kingdom of God. It's given to us, no strings attached; from God's perspective, it's our human right.

However, those who allow their rights and/or freedom to be taken away often don't realize they possess them in the first place.

They may feel pain at the loss, but they don't really know exactly what it is they've lost.

Before the new Christian can fully appreciate the kind of freedom that Christ bought on the cross, the "older and wiser" Christian comes along and starts quoting the rules. "Do this. Don't do that." Eager to learn everything about living the spiritual life, of course, the new Christian is quite grateful to be educated and learn the formula, never imagining that what he is giving up is not so much the "carnal nature" as he is told, but his freedom to choose—right from wrong, good from evil, light from dark. The formula he's given is not his at all. It's not even God's. It's one *person's* formula, the one this individual has made up as he's traveled his particular spiritual journey.

I have often wondered why God ever trusted us with such a potent force as freedom, when He knew that we'd cause damage to ourselves, to others, and to the planet because of never learning how to respect and honor it.

When I wake up in the morning, I have certain choices. I can choose to call an enemy and cuss her out, or I can choose to take a rifle and shoot at cars on the freeway. You have those choices, too.

On the other hand, I can have flowers sent to my friend (or enemy). I can stop to help someone stranded on the freeway. I can give my child a hug—even after he's been naughty. Again, these are our choices.

Passion adds another dimension to freedom in the area of our behavior. The person who is unaware that he has choices and is not in touch with his passion will not act on his impulses; nothing is driving him. The person who knows he has choices yet feels no passion likewise will not act on his impulses; again, he lacks motivation. The person who is unaware that he has choices but feels his passion is dangerous because he is often out of control.

So there is the most hope for the person who is aware that he has choices and is fully in touch with his passion— because he is constantly aware of the need to control his impulses and use his passion for good. Unlike the others, this person knows about the edge and has possibly even gone over it a few times. For this person, passionate freedom is something to be treasured first of all, and then to be explored in the context of God's watchful eye.

Those of us who went into the prison for the first time met at Red Robin for lunch between sessions.

"That was absolutely wonderful," I exclaimed, remembering the morning with the inmates. "I bet it's not as much fun, though, when you have to live there day in and day out."

"Yeah," one woman agreed. "It tends to lose something when you can't leave and go to Red Robin for lunch with your friends."

Of course. I could *choose* to leave the prison that day and go to Red Robin for lunch. The inmates ate in the cafeteria. And then, well, I love the hamburgers at Red Robin—passionately.

It would not surprise me in the least if an inmate at that prison who was in for twenty years and then released overdosed on hamburgers at Red Robin or steak at the Sizzler.

How do you suddenly handle both freedom and passion before you've discovered the edge?

Over the Edge

We go over the edge whenever we "feel free" to allow our passion(s) to drive us to destructive behaviors that hurt us or others. That ultimately hurts God.

Going over the edge was a general pastime for me a few years ago. Of course, I didn't know that's what I was doing. I didn't see the edge, let alone know I was tumbling over it. Even when I finally discovered it, all it did was scare me. I had no idea what to do. I had no idea it was possible to walk along it without falling over—to maintain a balancing act.

What does going over the passionate edge look like? It's simply this: when we take the gift of freedom, and then driven by the gift of passion, in our unredeemed and sinful state, we fly off the edge without a parachute. It's being out of control. It could happen for a moment, or we could fly over the edge and stay there several years. Some people never recover.

The awareness shouldn't cause us to live in terror of plunging over the edge. What it should do is cause us to absolutely thrust ourselves on God's mercy, praying for His keeping power moment by moment. That's all we can depend on—ever.

I can only talk about this because I've survived many tumbles, and I know there's plenty of hope for those who choose to wake up and fight for their freedom and the right to exercise their passion and who understand that life along the passionate edge is one of constant wakefulness because "your enemy the devil prowls around like a roaring lion looking for someone to devour" (1 Pet. 5:8).

I do believe that Satan is alive and well on planet earth and that he is the one who gives us that little extra shove over the edge, and then laughs.

I have felt him shove me as certainly as I've felt anything, and nothing makes me scramble back up over the edge quicker. I want nothing to do with him, his cohorts, or his kingdom.

I don't believe in giving him a lot of attention, but we do need to understand that he has an agenda for our lives. His agenda for us is the exact opposite of God's, and he knows that the best way to accomplish his agenda is to shove us over the edge, causing us to go out of control. Because it's when we're hurting the worst that we're the most desperate and open to his voice. He's passionate, too, about one thing—evil.

There. That's all the attention we're giving Satan in this book. The Bible says to stay alert to how he works and that's really all we need to do. Stay aware.

After going over the edge, if we don't give in to despair, we can move in one of two directions. We can either go for full spiritual recovery and God's redemption, or we can scramble back up and onto the edge and then keep running, never to venture near it again out of fear of another tumble.

Trapped in Reality

Going over the edge has a kind of numbing effect. When we wake up, we may suddenly see the full reality of our out-of-control behavior. If we haven't learned to trust in God's mercy and redemption—most often we haven't or we wouldn't be over the edge in the first place—we wake up absolutely terrified of who we are and what we're capable of.

We may start to gain control, but then we begin to strategize. We plan to make sure that never happens again—that we never sin again and most certainly never go over the edge again. We discipline ourselves, run around to all of our appointments, and claim we have full, abundant, and passionate lives. In reality, all we've done is fill our lives with a rigid and grueling schedule so that we can appease an angry God and try to balance out the guilt.

I know a guy, Dan, who unbeknownst to his wife, got involved in an adulterous and homosexual affair. When his marriage eventually broke up, understandably, he couldn't forgive himself for what he'd done.

Since all of this happened several years ago, to my knowledge he hasn't gone on one date. "I don't trust myself sexually," he told me. "How could I have done that? If I did that I could do it again. God can't trust me."

Dan is typical of many people who, once over the edge, never trust themselves again. They never take risks of any kind that might take them close to the edge. For Dan, a relationship equals sexual feelings which could lead to sin. He's trapped.

My friend, Rob, has also gone over the edge in the past. His way of dealing with his fear of the passionate edge is to keep his public image pure and unblemished. He guards every word that comes out of his mouth (you can actually see him mentally calculating each word before he speaks it). He even walks rigidly. His body erect, he moves deliberately and approaches others with caution. He holds himself back in conversation and relationships.

▼

Both Dan and Rob would say they don't trust themselves, that they're living "wisely." The truth is when we choose to "keep" ourselves rather than let God "keep" us, it's really God we don't trust.

The answer is not to choose to live rigid lives far from the passionate edge, far from the danger of tumbling off the edge into sin. Whether you believe it or not, there is a place of recovery that includes climbing right back on the horse and trusting once again.

Recovering

Recovery from a tumble off the edge can begin only when we take responsibility for the tumble and not make excuses like: "The horse was going too fast." "It was the wrong kind of saddle." "I haven't ridden in so long." Instead, we need to say, "Whoops. I fell off the horse."

Yes, I realize that our times over the edge are often much more than "whoops" and tumbles. They're more like devastating crashes.

Dan and Rob are not the only ones I've watched go over the edge. I remember my friend, Diane.

Diane was raised in a rigidly religious foster home, sexually abused by more than one authority figure, and she married at a young age. She began to loosen up and discover her freedom before she learned any responsibility. She ended up going over the edge many times in her marriage.

Fifteen years later her marriage ended in divorce. She began to grieve the loss of the relationship with her husband, and for a while she could not, would not trust any men. She would allow them to only get so close and then involuntarily she'd pull away.

But like the rest of us, she could only put off the recovery process for so long. After the grief work, she had to admit to her part of the responsibility in the failure of her marriage. Early on, she was too controlling, too perfectionistic, too rigid.

If passion has ever taken you over the edge, you know what I mean when I say that somewhere down deep you knew, even as you were going over, that something was terribly wrong and yet you chose to ignore all the signs. For those moments of turning our backs on God, we're responsible. We're responsible for ignoring all of the little nudges from God and loved ones. We are responsible for plunging ahead blindly at accelerated speeds so that we don't hear or see those on the sidelines holding up red flags. We are responsible for letting ourselves become so desperate that taking care of our pain and making ourselves happy becomes more of a priority to us than loving God and others and fitting into His redemptive plan. We are totally responsible.

Making ourselves aware of our responsibility is not for the purpose of beating ourselves over the head, nor is it so that we can play the role of martyr and especially not victim.

Exactly the opposite is true. Taking full responsibility for our plunges over the edge in the name of freedom is necessary so that we don't get stuck the rest of our lives in the rut of martyr or victim. As much good as the recovery movement has done, I feel like we got stuck halfway through. Too many of us were only willing to recover so that we might take the edge off of our pain and feel better.

Those of us in the recovery movement have talked a lot about how, when, where, and by whom we were victimized. But as we progress on the journey of healing, we need to move our focus off of the past and onto the present and future, so that we might become the passionate and redemptive "lights" God needs in this dark world. God's purposes are never about the individual alone, but about spreading the good news through passionate love and redemption. His purposes are always about relationship and community.

I believe in recovery from victimization. I'm so thankful that victims of all kinds have places and groups where they can receive support, encouragement, and solid healing from addictions and abusive relationships. But I also believe that the only

▼

kind of true recovery happens when we understand God's ultimate redemptive plan.

A big part of that plan is learning to walk freely along the passionate edge so that we don't go over and end up hurting ourselves or others.

Feeling for the Edge

It's a precarious balancing act, but we can learn to do it.

I love challenges. I no longer dine at all-you-can-eat restaurants. (My children beg me to take them, but I can usually talk them into something else.) I no longer dine at all-you-can-eat restaurants because that is exactly what I do once I'm there. I eat all I can eat—spaghetti, salad, mashed potatoes, rolls, macaroni and cheese, corn, fried chicken, and five kinds of desserts piled a foot high on my plate. I have no control.

My daughter can keep a piece of chocolate in her bedroom, in plain sight, for weeks. One time she kept a piece of solid milk chocolate Halloween candy on her dresser until the following March.

I don't understand this kind of person. The smallest taste of any kind of chocolate sets off cravings in me like you wouldn't believe. I've never actually done it, yet, but I know I could easily gobble up an entire box—no matter how large—of chocolates in one sitting. The point isn't how large the box is or how I might feel afterwards, but that as long as there is even one chocolate left in that box, I salivate and can't stop thinking about it until it's gone. It's the same with a chocolate cake.

Actually my addiction to chocolate and food in general is a rather minor over-the-edge area in my life when I consider some of the things I struggle with since I've let myself become passionately alive.

Well, then, really, we might wonder, *why even bother with the passionate life? Isn't it kind of a hassle?*

Stay with me. For you see, without passion, I don't even get to *taste* the chocolate. My sense of taste is gone. I may *hear* sound but no music because I can't hear notes. I may *see* a bunch of flowers as I walk along a garden path, but I don't see the beads of dew on each tiny pink rosebud—my vision's a blur. The *smells* all blend together—I can't distinguish cinnamon from bayberry. I may feel like someone is hugging me when I'm really being strangled. I can't tell the difference.

Life without passion? No thanks.

We have no guarantees. I can't guarantee that to walk along the passionate edge means never falling over, not for me, you, or anyone else. There are no formulas. There are no fences high enough, deep enough, or solid enough to hold us. If we want to go over, we'll go over.

No, the only way we learn to walk along the passionate edge is to do it, to take the risk—every day, every hour, every moment—alone, with others, and with God.

I'm learning to balance, to try new steps until I find my rhythm. I've tried eating just one chocolate at a time. It doesn't work, so I don't keep chocolate in the house. But I can go out, buy one piece, eat it, and come home. That works.

You'll find your rhythm, too. What works for you on the edge? Don't be afraid to try out new steps. That's the only way you'll discover your own rhythm.

My children think my life is boring because I enjoy a much calmer life than before. We have far fewer crises since I've learned to walk along the edge. I'm more content. Oh, I can still get wild and crazy, but not in a destructive way. For example, I think my daughter and I may go get little tattoos on our ankles this week, but that's about as crazy as it gets.

Our only hope for life on the passionate edge is that of awakening to His presence with us and knowing that for every step we take, He takes two. We must honor our freedom, and we can feel safe in doing so because God is always just a little bit ahead of us.

ELEVEN

▼

COMING OF AGE

Many people live responsibly in certain areas of behavior, but that doesn't necessarily mean these folks are responsible persons. Those of us raised in the sixties learned to challenge authority and break the rules. In the sixties, even the natural-born responsible people had to work hard at living responsibly because to do so wasn't "cool" back then.

I've noticed that living responsibly seems to come more easily for pre-baby boomers than it does for me. Sometimes I envy them. Sometimes. I also notice that they often have to work harder at living passionately than do those of my generation.

James Dean started some kind of trend, I think. The fifties child thought about it while the sixties child jumped on it. The fifties child was already living responsibly before even being presented with passion as a lifestyle choice, but the sixties child moved quickly to the passionate edge and leaped off, bypassing responsibility completely. Now we are paying for that impulsive leap because some of us never have learned responsibility.

My generation lifted themselves to a perpetual high, never imagining the consequences that awaited them. I don't blame the nineties adolescent for the rampant sex, violence, and drugs in our country today. My generation is simply reaping what we've sown.

It's important that we understand our generational programming in the area of responsibility so that as we begin to live on the passionate edge, we can do so responsibly.

When God gives us a gift, which I believe passion to be, it's our responsibility to honor that gift. To honor the gift of passion we must understand how fragile it is.

Poof!

Our passion for life can drift away seemingly almost on a whim, but it's really for any number of reasons: boredom, tiredness, inattentiveness, real or false guilt, pursuit of money, legalism, or routines.

When we lose our focus of what's really important, loving God and people, passion is gone. It ebbs away without our even realizing it. Before we know it, we're caught up in a quality of life that may even dole out a measure of success and satisfaction but no passion. We become only a shell of our former selves.

Being a man and human, Jesus must have had days when He was tempted to say to Himself, "Oh, I give up. I think I'll just sit down under this fig tree and take the day off."

And the next day.
      And the day after that.
            Passion ebbing. Losing it.

I look at Jesus' life and see a man who lived every single day with incredible passion, whether He was chasing the money changers out of the temple or teaching His disciples what it really meant to follow Him. He took responsibility for His passion every single day He lived on this earth. He was a man with a

▼

mission. He never stopped following His passion, not even for the briefest moment.

Knowing how easy it is to lose our passion should make us stop and take a serious look at what we're doing. Are we sacrificing our passion in any way at all? Is it worth it? What was it Jesus said about the man who gained the whole world, yet forfeited his soul? "Or what can a man give in exchange for his soul?" (Mark 8:36–37).

Our passion is at the very core of our soul. When we decide that no matter what we will possess our passion, it is our choice whether we use that passion for good or evil.

Passionate Evil

Evil is a strong word. Do we need to discuss it in a Christian book on the subject of Christian passion? I wish it weren't true, but I have known and do know "spiritual" people who use their passion to control, manipulate, and abuse others—often all in the name of "Christian love."

Now not too many of us would admit to using our passion for evil, but how do you think those who do ever got to that point. They had to start somewhere. They took small steps at first.

Lenore was the leader of a large Christian ministry in the South. An aggressive and powerful individual, she would call her employees into her office regularly to check their attitudes.

"Can't you see how your attitude is affecting the ministry?" she would berate them. "You need to repent of this immediately." Then she would take a "caring" stance before them, placing her hands on their shoulders, and pray for God's mercy on their devious hearts, bitter attitudes, or slanderous tongues.

These regular repentance sessions enabled her to maintain her position of power over her employees—all because she "cared" for the ministry and the "spiritual" growth of her employees.

One time in a marketing meeting, she got excited about the possibility of selling a large number of books, videos, and tapes at a conference.

"If we can just get someone who's read the book to stand up and tell how it changed her life—you know, saved her marriage, kept her from committing suicide, whatever, if we can get her to cry . . . I've seen it happen. We can sell five thousand books in fifteen minutes," she explained.

Exploit a crowd's emotions and make a lot of money. I call that using passion for evil.

Then there's David who has a ministry to parents. He tours the country, holds huge crusades, and quotes statistics about today's youth, your children and mine, that would spike your hair and turn it purple in a moment. He gives parents the horrible statistics, and just when you're pulling at your purple hair, frantic about whether your wayward teenager can ever be rescued, David saves the day. He says "The answers are all in my new book, . . ."

He also just happens to have with him copies of his other books and several videos and tapes, "just in case you're interested." Parents trample each other to snatch up copies of David's "answer-book" before they're all gone.

No, I'm not convinced that either Lenore or David set out to exploit and manipulate. If asked, they would claim a "calling" to do what they're doing, a burden for women, parents, prisoners, or whomever.

They're full of passion for their cause, no doubt about it. So what makes it evil. They've taken their passion over the edge and are using it to exploit our pain and profit monetarily.

Those are people in the public eye. Could that ever happen to you or me. Are we really capable of using our passion for evil? Every time we spank a child out of uncontrolled anger. Every time we let our grief over a loss turn to bitterness. Every time we put other people down because of jealousy over their successes and achievements.

I'm guilty of all of the above.

▼

I feel passion about many things, but I'm over the edge whenever I try to force my passion on others through coercive guilt or through any other method.

We may feel passionate about abortion. That does not give us the right to go out and kill those who perform abortions, as some deceived and ambitious vigilantes seem to think. "So, if you think you are standing firm, be careful that you don't fall!" (1 Cor. 10:12). It all comes down to the issues of the heart: insecurity, feelings of powerlessness, fear, deep burning rage, unresolved jealousy, and repressed grief.

Passion is like the elements. Like fire, it can warm or it can annihilate. Like water, passion can quench our thirst or it can pull us under and drown us.

We must lay our passion(s) before God continually, asking Him to purify them so that we might use them for His kingdom and good.

Tightening the Reins

Before we can use our passions for good, we must tighten the reins on the evil that pulls at us, and we can only do this for ourselves.

Parents may lecture incessantly about celibacy and abstinence to their teenagers; they feel strongly about it. They want their children to remain sexually pure, but then they climb into bed with a warm spouse. Do they even try to remember what it means to resist sexual temptation?

I can't help wondering if those who so easily keep all the rules, expecting others to do so as well, are even in touch with reality—their longings, dreams, feelings, and their passions. Unless I see them struggle with their own issues of passion, I tend to tune them out.

So whenever I see a strongly disciplined person who is rigidly adhering to a list of pet rules and trying to get everyone else to adhere to them, too, I'm suspicious. Is this person touching his or her passions. Every day. We can't just decide to tighten the reins and then discipline ourselves. It's not that simple.

For years I struggled to harness my own, my childrens' and everyone else's passions, thinking that was my mission.

It didn't work. I just ended up frustrated, constantly feeling deprived, and went over more edges than I could keep track of. Everyone kept getting mad at me for getting into their business.

Have you ever noticed that the harder we try to control something, the more out of control it becomes? The way to gain weight is to try not to gain weight.

Well, if trying to control our passions so that we don't use them for evil doesn't work, then what does? How can we accomplish this if trying doesn't work? For me, it started with one step, one decision, and one commitment, for one day.

The Alchoholics Anonymous folks know what they're talking about when they say, "One day at a time." That's all we have. That's the most we can hope to control at any one time—today.

We often arrive at this conclusion through a series of failures, setbacks, and mistakes. One thing I've learned about God over the years is that He does not support us in our extremes, of any kind. When we move into an extreme, we do so without God.

Now I don't mean we lose His presence, but we lose His support. He waits for us on the edge. When we *fail to tighten our own reins, God is faithful to tighten them for us.*

God promises to bring good out of what Satan intends for evil. The one good thing about extremes is that they are a constant reminder of our humanness, our inability to stay in control without God. We *need* Him. We will always *need* Him. We were created to *need* Him.

Kurt Cobain, lead singer of the popular Seattle band Nirvana, took on a huge responsibility when his band became famous. As a role model, he was responsible to all of his young fans to take an aggressive stance against drugs, oppose violence, and celebrate life.

In his last moments of life, he violated all three of the above. Cobain was a man of extremes, I think it's safe to say. In the end, his extremes killed him. I wasn't there, but I would guess that he was fresh out of hope that God would meet him on the edge.

Cobain was a man in touch with his passion. His songs were full of emotion—anger, fear, and bitter sorrow—but he failed to take responsibility, to tighten the reins, to commit his passion to good and God.

The commitment, the decision we must make, if we are to responsibly live in touch with our passions, is to use them not for evil but for good.

We think of Kurt Cobain as a tragic figure now, but we can't lose sight of those, even in this same industry, who are now taking their responsibility seriously. Steven Tyler of the band Aerosmith is one. A heavy drug user for many years, he cleaned up his act and is now speaking out publicly against drugs.

Just making the decision, of course, does not guarantee success, but sometimes I think the intensity with which we pursue our passions is in direct proportion to our rate of failure. We will fail to do good sometimes and do evil instead, but failure is a positive sign; it means we're trying. God is more interested in the purity of the motivations of our hearts than He is in the success rate of our ability to keep our commitment to do good.

So we make the decision to tighten the reins day by day and moment by moment so that we might use our passion responsibly, not for evil, but for good. What does that really mean?

Passionate Good

I recently read a story on the front page of *The Seattle Times* about a state employment counselor who spends hours of her free time every week typing resumes on her personal computer, making connections, and offering free advice—all for her clients, many of whom are homeless. "Jo Ann is dedicated to helping people," her boss said. "She is not what the public typically thinks of as a state employee," someone using her strengths, her job, and her passion for good. At the bottom of the same page is an article on O. J. Simpson.

As the editor of a parenting magazine, I love to publish stories about children doing good stuff. Recently, we ran a story about a boy, who in eight years as a sea turtle volunteer, has saved the lives of fifteen thousand loggerhead hatchlings, an endangered species. We ran another story about a candystriper who rides in the back of an ambulance on a regular basis to hold a hand and offer an encouraging word. Another story was about a boy who helped raise $1,000 to build a playground for handicapped children. These are teens who are already learning what it means to use their passion for good.

Every day is a new day to help someone, to reach out and care, and to love with everything we've got—and with everything God's given us.

Remember when you got your driver's license? You accepted the responsibility to drive in such a way as not to endanger the lives of others. One reason people get more than a little upset when someone is killed by a drunk driver is because the guilty party has acted irresponsibly—to the point of taking another's life.

Jesus went about doing good. It was His responsibility in coming to earth to use His passion for redemption and good—to redeem, to save, and to heal.

That may be the most important reason for you to discover your unique purpose on the planet. If Jesus' purpose was to die on the cross and redeem humankind and if He expects us to play a part in that purpose, wouldn't it be a good idea for us to go about the business of finding out specifically how each of us fits into the plan?

If we really do want to be a growing people and part of God's redemptive plan, we can make specific decisions to be an encourager, love our world, forgive those who hurt us, walk in integrity, and share our faith without shame.

Now, as I already mentioned, making the decision doesn't mean automatic success in keeping our commitment, but our decision to use our passion for God is an automatic invitation to God to please involve Himself in helping us find the strength to keep our commitment. My experience is that that's exactly what He does.

"I can't forgive Merilee [my fifteen-year-old] one more time," I will cry out after an especially painful conflict. I'll pray, cry, scream, rant, and rave. "God, help me."

Maybe not immediately, but at some point my heart begins to turn and fill with compassion toward a child who is simply trying to grow up.

God is with me because I've made a decision to forgive. I want this to be my constant stance toward those who hurt me.

Passion is a gift, remember. Let's accept it graciously. Let's learn to honor it.

Honoring the Gift

Honor means different things to different people. What it means to me is respect, to hold in high esteem, to cherish, to care for, and to celebrate.

Honoring the gift of passion can mean any number of things. It can mean:

▼ following God's call no matter where it leads;

▼ refusing to indulge yourself sexually;

▼ holding your temper so you don't punch someone;

▼ making hard decisions, say, between loyalty and integrity when you can't have both;

▼ or celebrating an ocean wave, a sunrise, or the gift of life.

I suppose that for someone who's experienced death, even in the abstract, the honoring of life is a privilege unequal to anything else. I celebrate my passion because I'm so grateful to be alive. Sometimes I balk at the responsibility it invokes because the dark side of me would like to indulge myself in carnal activity for the rest of my days. But I know the destruction that carnal passion can cause. I'll take the responsibility. I'll honor the gift.

When a friend of mine was dying of cancer a few years ago I remember celebrating life with her one day and grieving her passing the next. Honoring the gift means ultimately making one commitment—living each day and each moment of life to the fullest. That is the ultimate responsiblity of those who choose to live on the passionate edge.

———

TWELVE

▼

A SHARPER EDGE

What do you do when you're on a mountain in an ice cave, hear a thunderous roar, and realize it's an avalanche? Before you can think or scramble for safety, you're engulfed in complete darkness. My friend's son, along with two of his friends, recently experienced the horror of this scenario. As one might expect, the young men were terrified. Hundreds, maybe thousands of pounds of snow lay on top of and around them. Why even think about survival? There was no surviving something like this.

Then one of the men pulled a small knife out of his pocket. "Hey, I have a pocketknife."

"So?" his two buddies said glumly and in unison.

"OK, what were your ideas?" he asked his friends.

Thus began the arduous task of digging out of the avalanche with a pocketknife. Hour after hour, they knelt on one another's shoulders and chipped away at the snow with the little knife.

Discouragement set in, but then, finally, there was a teeny bit of light. As they continued to chip away, the hole of light became larger. Eventually they dug themselves out.

In an article in *Delicious* magazine, Kathryn Arnold writes this about creativity:

> The most crucial factor in creativity is . . . intrinsic motivation or passion. Creativity is impossible without that inner spark. People are more likely to be creative if they're intrinsically motivated. That means they're captivated by what they're doing. They find it enjoyable, satisfying, and personally challenging.
>
> Finding or discovering what impassions you then giving yourself permission to explore those things is the key to reclaiming your creative spirit. Numerous self-help books teach creative thinking skills; however, intrinsic motivation is not something that can be learned. It comes from within. Try to remember what excited you as a child or think about what intrigues you now. Then allow yourself the time and resources to develop skill in these areas.[1]

I think we could safely say the guys in the avalanche were passionately motivated, so they were able to find a creative solution. In this case, their creativity saved their lives. Are you passionately motivated? To do what? To be whom?

I've heard too many people say, "I'm just not creative." Maybe a more accurate statement would be, "I'm just not motivated." Or, "I just lack passion for that." Lacking passion and/or motivation in one area doesn't mean you lack it in all areas, although it can. Life on the passionate edge sets us up for discovering what it is we naturally possess creativity for.

Openness

According to psychologist Abraham Maslow and other experts, the creative personality is determined by several things:

1. High amounts of energy, enthusiasm, and a general zest for living

2. A well-developed sense of humor and the ability to laugh at yourself

3. A high level of tolerance for uncertainty and ambiguity

4. A problem or project orientation

5. A need for and ability to make productive use of solitude

6. Independent thinking and a tendency to question conventional wisdom

7. Openness to new ideas

8. Playfulness

9. Willingness to risk failure and to be different

10. The ability to withhold judgment

11. A general openness to the environment[2]

You may read this list and not see yourself at all. You may see several friends, but this is definitely not you. Don't be alarmed. Don't give up; this personality is not one that people are necessarily born with. Some of us may have natural tendencies in some of these areas, but I can honestly say that other than number six, I possessed none of the above until I discovered the passionate side of life. I believe the discovery of my passionate self is what ignited any creativity I've developed over the last few years.

Every item on the list falls under one heading—openness. As Christians, we're often afraid of openness because we think God has one way of looking at things and it's all in the Bible. We can even quote chapter and verse if there's ever a question on a particular issue. So what good is openness? We fear accidentally inviting something into our lives that is not of God.

Christian television is the perfect example. I have often wondered why when I tune into Christian television that I see only one of two things—preaching or singing. Certainly God's people should be the most creative people on earth. I should be able to choose from drama, comedy, vocal concerts, humor, instrumental concerts, talk shows, documentaries, news broadcasts, intellectual as well as spiritual interviews, romance, and more.

We feel safe with preaching and singing and can't go wrong. It's a safe way to communicate, and, at least most of the time, people will applaud our efforts.

We're often afraid to open ourselves up to anything different because we feel we won't be able to control what we're opening ourselves up to. What we must remember, though, is that the act of opening ourselves doesn't at all mean we have to accept whatever shows up. We can reject anything at any time. All openness does is provide opportunity for the Holy Spirit to move in a fresh way in our lives.

If you feel lacking in the creative department, it may be that you simply need to learn to open up in the areas in which you've locked yourself away.

Once convinced we need to open up, how do we go about actually doing that? I remember the day it began to happen for me. A mentor-friend and I were driving down the street.

"Well, I really did some repenting this week," she said. "I feel like such a sinner." Then she went on to tell me what it was she needed to repent of, but I was hardly listening. She had said she was a "sinner"? I'd been programmed for the last several years to believe that one couldn't be both a Christian *and* a sinner. You were either a Christian *or* a sinner. When you became a Christian you stopped sinning, I was taught, therefore you were no longer a "sinner." It sounds so crazy to me now after all of these years, but I believed it then because I trusted, without "questioning conventional wisdom." I wasn't open to any other way of thinking.

And now, here was a sane person, a dear friend I'd grown to love, trust, and admire, saying something entirely different. What was I supposed to think? Believe? Do? Was she crazy? Wrong? Misled? Or was I? Was she or was she not a sinner? Was I? Did it matter?

The way it turned out, it mattered a great deal because as I *opened* myself up to hear more from her, it ended up revolutionizing my entire Christian experience. I'd become a Christian many years before, but I can't say that I actually started growing in my spiritual journey until that day. How can we grow when we think we've arrived, that we're beyond reproach, no longer a sinner, perfect even?

I had to listen to her. She'd already proven her spiritual maturity to me in many ways before now.

We open up by asking just one scary question. Someone says something we have never heard before, something we may even consider quite bizarre, something we may wish we had never heard.

The first question, maybe the best one to ask, is, "What kind of insight can I gain here? Is there a truth here for me?" Then watch out. Because once we learn that we can indeed question, open and grow, the passionate life becomes the most exciting and, indeed, daring adventure you can possibly imagine and the most intense as it drives us forward in our creative endeavors.

Pacing Ourselves

I figure if you've done something once, that's enough. I get bored easily. I thrive on creativity, creative solutions to problems, creative ways of thinking about old ideas, and creative ways to approach life.

It can frustrate those around me, especially dyed-in-the-wool traditionalists who thrive on rituals. Those are people who like things just the way they are and who make it their mission in life to make sure people like me don't try to sneak in and change anything.

I got a new job in an editorial office once and within a week I wanted to change everything they were doing. I didn't know at that time that there was a tactful and diplomatic way to suggest new ideas or concepts. I just blurted stuff out.

"We need a different rejection letter to send to writers," I told the other editor in my department, the one who'd written the rejection letter we were using. "One that's more helpful," I said. "We need a line of books for teens," I continued. "The workload is overwhelming. We need an assistant."

Any kind of a problem, at least what I considered to be a problem, needed a creative solution, right? I was open to anything that would work . . . now.

My boss and coworkers weren't. They'd worked there longer, understood the system and the budget a lot better than I did. By the way, nothing kills creativity like systems and budgets. Left-brain thinkers love systems and budgets. I guess maybe they can find a way to be creative within the system and budget, but I don't know how they do it.

Sometimes my passion wears me out, and I'm no fool. I know that sometimes it wears out those around me—my loved ones, friends, and relatives. I really feel sorry for those people I used to work with. I don't know how they stood my continual hyperventilating about change all the time.

It's just that I have all of these ideas and I keep trying to change the world and actually think I can—every single day. It's enough to wear anyone out, even me.

Because I'm such a believer in celebrating the process, whatever it is we're doing, I no longer burn myself out to reach a destination. The story of Moses and the promised land used to discourage me until I realized that he must have learned this little secret, too. He wandered in the wilderness for forty years with only a promise to keep him moving toward his goal. A promise from God, I might add. The Israelites would reach the promised land, but after Moses died.

Moses had to have learned that the destination is not the ultimate goal. The beauty in the painting is found in the painter's openness, passion, and ability to celebrate the process during the creating. I believe only those who know how to celebrate the process succeed in their creative endeavors.

Pacing is truly only a concern if we haven't learned to passionately celebrate our creativity. People go see doctors every day to learn how to slow down, to prevent heart attacks caused from working too hard and too fast, and to learn what they need to do to pace themselves.

I'm learning to listen to my body. I don't need a doctor to tell me when I need to slow down. When I'm no longer celebrating but just going through the motions, everything begins to suffer. It's something we can feel if we're paying attention.

I'm in an extremely difficult situation at the moment that drains me of energy very quickly whenever I have to deal with it. It won't ever go away—that's a settled fact. I'm definitely not celebrating this situation and consequently am unable to be creative in the midst of it. So I'm learning to pace myself in the way I deal with it, and in the meantime, do some soul work. Examine my beliefs about it. Pray that God will show me ways to celebrate it, and not only celebrate it, but celebrate it passionately. One day I know my creativity will spring to life in the midst of it. I just hope the end result doesn't take forty years, but if it does, I will have been what God asked me to be during the process—a passionate, creative celebrator. Obviously, part of the creative process is learning to problem solve.

Creative Problem-solving

When we're first learning to live on the passionate edge, it seems like all we can do is feel. Feelings rush up in us faster than we can process what they mean, so we don't always make it to the rational side of the problem, whatever it is, the side that is able to step back, take a somewhat objective look, and consider the options. The creative personality sees each problem not as an obstacle but as a new challenge, something to be conquered.

With five teenagers, as you might imagine, new problems descend on me on a daily basis. If I crumbled with each one, I'd be a mess. Well, I was, before the passionate edge. Each new problem drained me. Things are different now. First, I *feel* the problem, then I *look* at it and try to solve it.

Something, a new problem, hit our family a few days ago. Actually, I have known it was a problem for a long time, but because I didn't have to deal with it directly, I could ignore it. Then recently, it appeared in front of my face, and I couldn't ignore it.

At first, all I could do was cry for hours, so long and so hard that I woke up one day and my eyes were almost swollen shut.

"God, this is horrible," I cried, "and there's not a thing I can do about it."

I thought it would never quit hurting. I always think that, but I grieved fully and now the sharp pain is gone. The ache is there, but whereas sharp pain hinders clear thinking, aches are good motivators.

Now I have to solve this problem, at least my part of it. So I ask myself the following questions:

1. What is God requiring of me? (What am I accountable for?)

2. How do I love the other people involved in this problem? (How can I hold them accountable?)

3. Practically, how do I live now with this problem until it resolves itself, it if ever does?

This problem may go away, but then again it may not. It has to do with addiction. Addictions don't always go away, and they never go away easily.

Creativity on the passionate edge means tackling this problem, hitting it head on in ways that may surprise me. Some days I'll lay low; other days I'll hit it full force. On the passionate edge we can't become weary of doing good because God's mercies are new every morning and creative—always creative.

Addictions are never bigger than God's creative love. There is no problem too difficult, no problem beyond his redemption.

One thing about life on the passionate edge, there is always, always, always hope—a new way of looking at something, a new approach, a new day. What keeps it all interesting is that often the solution to the problem is exactly the opposite of what we might expect. God truly is full of surprises.

Spend It—Don't Save It

"Ten tips on saving time."

"Ten tips on saving money."

"Ten tips on saving energy."

Everything is save, save, save. Everywhere we turn, we are told how to save something. If we really saved everything we're told to save, there would be no room to move, and we'd have no fun because saving is responsible, practical, and mature, and spending is reckless, spontaneous, and fun.

Yeah, I know there needs to be a balance, but since all we hear is how to save, let's talk a little about how to spend. The very nature of God is that of sharing, spending, and sowing. The Bible is full of stories about giving something away.

So how did we ever buy into this saving idea? It's because as humans, we're forever seeking ways to feel more secure—car insurance, life insurance, fire insurance, cancer insurance, renter's/owner's insurance. In case we ever lose anything, we want to have a guarantee we'll get it back. We wouldn't want to be without whatever it is.

I'm that way. The only thing I can really handle losing and never finding again is pounds off my body.

I'm suggesting we rethink what we've been taught about saving. How can we creatively spend more time, more money, more energy? For isn't that what life on the passionate edge is all about? I have a secret theory: I think a lot of our stress comes from trying to figure out how we can save more money, time, and energy. If we quit worrying about it so much, we could relax and be more effective in our roles in God's kingdom.

When we get up in the mornings and write out our to-do lists, how about focusing on how we're going to spend our time rather than struggle with how we can save a minute here and there by doubling up on errands? Focusing on spending instead of saving puts us more in the moment. We begin to realize how precious each moment is, that we'll never again live this mo-

▼

ment. We can focus on celebrating the moments instead of hoarding the minutes.

How can I creatively spend my money today? One of my favorite memories was the day I left work early, grabbed my five children, and headed into the city to spend as much money as we could. Well, as much money as we had, which that day happened to be about eighty dollars. The kids were little: we bought balloons, ice cream cones, and chinese food. We went to the aquarium, the movies, and the wharf, and when the money was all gone, we came home.

The bills got paid, maybe a little late, but no one had a heart attack over it.

Spending money is fun, have you ever noticed? What if just once you bought something because you wanted it and didn't even look at how much it cost? What a revolutionary thought.

What? You don't have any money? C'mon, look again. If you have ten dollars, you have money. The money has to go for bread and milk, cheese and eggs? So what if you went without bread and milk, cheese and eggs just this once? What if you went to the used bookstore instead and bought every family member a book? What if you rented three movies and watched them all in one night? Or splurged on a bouquet of flowers for the dining room table—a gift from you to you?

By the way, creative spending is addictive. If you go over the edge here, refer to chapter 10 and climb your way back up. Living on the passionate edge is about "carpe diem."

Seizing the Day

A friend of mine, Lynne, did some creative and serious seizing of the day at a Michael Bolton concert recently. If you don't know who Michael Bolton is, you can't fully appreciate this story. If you know who he is, this story will send you into serious swooning and, hopefully, creatively seizing passionate moments of your own.

Michael Bolton had sung a few songs and then the lights were dimmed. A moment later when the lights came back on, he stood in the aisle, only a couple of feet from my friend! Two monstrous bodyguards stood on either side while he sang his heart out.

So my friend, a passionate on-the-edge "seizer" if I've ever known one, said to herself, *I'll never get this chance again.*

So she reached out, lightly touched Michael Bolton's arm, and before the bodyguards could jump in and ruin everything, he turned to Lynne, took her hand, looked straight into her eyes, and sang "Georgia on My Mind" as if she were the only woman in the whole building. Her name is Lynne, not Georgia, but she didn't really care.

Wow, how's that for seizing the day? The moment?

The Bible calls it "making the most of every opportunity" (Eph. 5:16). OK, Paul may not have been thinking about rock concerts, but I suppose we can apply it to any situation. It's developing the mental attitude that says, "How can I creatively seize this moment and make it matter? What is this moment offering me?" Then it's grabbing the moment by the gut.

If you're in the process of developing a creative personality, you won't have to wonder how this happens and you won't have to try to make anything happen. Creative seizing of the day will happen because your eyes are finally open and you're *seeing* the day. Those moments were always there for you to grab—you just never saw them before, let alone thought about grabbing them and making them yours.

It's not at all difficult. There's really only a couple of things you have to remember about creatively seizing the day:

▼ Leave your house—you have to get out where things are happening.

▼ Seize the day—once you're out, don't observe, participate. Go for it, whatever it is.

It's just too incredibly and wonderfully simple, isn't it?

———

THIRTEEN

▼

REIGNITING YOUR DREAMS

The French novelist Anaïs Nin wrote in her diary:

> Dreams pass into the reality of action. From the action stems the dream again; and this interdependence produces the highest form of living.[1]

Only those who live on the passionate edge can ever achieve their dreams because it takes passion to drive the kind of confidence that drives the kind of action that turns dreams into reality. Passion is a motivator like no other. It surges beneath the surface, ready to spring into motion whenever we extend an invitation. I constantly feel it bubbling, prodding, and pushing everything I do of any significance, anything that really matters.

Jesus Christ exploded quietly onto the scene two thousand years ago with one purpose in mind—to redeem and heal us from sin. That's still His purpose today.

As His followers, our dream is patterned after His—we are to live our lives and achieve our dreams so as to redeem and heal humanity from sin. If we're living our lives for any other reason, we're off track. We are people with a mission.

With that in mind, how does your specific dream fit into the overall plan? My thirteen-year-old daughter and I have a new dream. She mentioned once that she'd like to travel to every state in the country. I thought about it and now I'm saying, "Why not?"

Our plan is to move next year to a small condo, a place to hang our hats basically, and then once a month travel to one of the fifty states. Maybe we'll have a plan, or maybe we'll just close our eyes and put our finger on the map. By the time she's eighteen, we plan to have traveled to all fifty states.

As a responsible pursuer of passion and a participant in God's plan of redemption, I must ask, what good is all of that traveling going to do anyone? If it was so that Amber and I could have a good time, it wouldn't do much good at all. But I plan on meeting people, doing volunteer work, and integrating ourselves into wherever we are. My goal is for this dream to be redemptive, to fit into the overall plan. My passion for adventure is driving it as well as my passion to enlarge my daughter's view of the world.

In an earlier chapter, I mentioned my desire to become a nun, the only way I knew to get close enough to God, as close as I wanted to be. Was that a dream? At sixteen, maybe it was. All I can say is I'm so grateful that dream didn't become a reality. I know for a fact I would be one miserable person.

But my dream at nine years old, of one day becoming a writer, has become a reality. I'm living this dream ecstatically.

I'm always looking for new dreams, resurrecting, and adjusting old ones to see if they fit living current ones. This is the mode I'm in since I discovered how our dreams fit into life on the passionate edge. What if that's not your mode? Maybe your dreams died a long time ago, and you're having a real struggle finding them, or finding anything new to dream about. You certainly don't feel like you're living your dream. It's more like a stinky kind of reality.

What now? How do you begin to dream again? How do you recover that past dream? How do you make your dream become a reality?

Touching Your Dreams

What did you dream about being, and what did you dream about doing as a child? As a preteen? As a young adult? Did you ever role-play? Who were you? Shirley Temple? Roy Rogers? Zorro? (Uh-oh, my age is showing.) Luke Skywalker? Oprah Winfrey? The president of the United States?

Once we've chosen to live on the passionate edge, touching our dreams is very possible. All it takes is a little imagination, a little confidence, and a little energy. When you're driven by passion, this is no problem. To touch your dream is to bring it up, remember it, and ponder it a while so that the longing kicks in once again.

Sometimes we're afraid to remember our dreams because we can't really believe we can ever make them happen. Remembering them only depresses us. As a young girl, you dreamed of singing in front of thousands. Now you have to turn the shower on full blast so your family won't hear you and laugh their heads off. As a young boy, you dreamed of acting in science fiction films like *Star Trek,* but the truth is, you don't even understand how to work a computer.

What happened? Your dream could be one voice or acting lesson away, one step away from turning a dream into reality.

I watched a woman I worked with move step by step, day by day out of a dead-end job. Every day she did just one thing on her job search—made one phone call or wrote one letter. Prior to this I had watched her make one other important move—I had watched her begin to wake up out of a long sleep—she came to life before my eyes. She entered into therapy, into pain, and ultimately into life on the passionate edge.

After one year of daily steps, she courageously quit the dead-end job she'd had for at least ten years and is now working

▼

at a better company doing more of what she really wants to do. She is almost ready to transition from that company into a job that fits her even better. She is making her dream job come true. It all started with a passionate belief in herself.

When we dream, we break down barriers, we fly without wings, and we run without feet. We sing without voices, and we fight fires without water. Anything is possible—anything at all. That's the only rule we have to consider—no limits. God might allow anything to happen if we're willing to dream.

The first step toward touching your dream is to (1) remember, and then (2) ponder until you feel the longing.

Remember

One hindrance to remembering is the tendency to judge the desire or dream before it takes hold in your mind. Immediately upon recalling the dream, before any feeling can register, our mind takes us to: "How silly. That was a childish dream born in a childish mind. Eject." Or, "Ridiculous. I could never do (be) that. Why, it would take thousands of dollars (years of college) to even come close to doing (being) that. Impossible."

At these times your mind becomes the enemy. It refuses to cooperate because it's programmed in the same way a computer is programmed, but a computer can be reprogrammed. We have to reprogram our minds.

After many, many times of reprogramming, my mind agrees with me now more often than not. I create a dream, and it says, "I can do that. I can be that." As long as my heart is committed to God, my mind knows I can do or be anything.

Now, just for the sake of clarification, that doesn't mean there aren't people out there who are not committed to God yet are doing great things. I believe the difference lies in the results of the fruit of our labors. Are we leading people into a closer relationship with God on their spiritual journeys? Or, are we leading them to destruction?

I heard Mother Teresa say recently on her eighty-fourth birthday, when asked for a message to the people, that she had

▼

no message and was "quite tired of giving messages." Mother Teresa doesn't have to give a message anymore. She *is* a message. Her passion inspires my passion for good.

On the other hand, I was in a record store a few days ago and felt sick to my stomach when the lyrics of a certain song which was being pumped through the intercom system registered inside of my head. I can't imagine how the members of that band can live with themselves. They may have a gift for music. They may even be successful financially, but where are they leading their listeners?

I'll have to admit I wish some people *wouldn't* remember their dreams. We'd all be better off—all the more reason for those of us who follow Christ to get a move on, remember our dreams, and inspire our world for God.

Ponder

At first memory, like I mentioned above, our minds move through all kinds of various gymnastics before we can ever accomplish anything. That's why we must master the art of pondering. Pondering takes us into that place of feeling, of passionate longing for our lost dreams, and for lives that pulsate with purpose and meaning. We must stay in this place a while so that the longing takes hold, begins to form images, and starts to imagine how a dream might become a reality.

We will never touch our dreams without remembering and pondering. Over the years many of our dreams have died. Even as we remember our dreams, before we have a grip on them and can make anything happen, they die again. This is as it should be.

Letting Your Dreams Die

"Unless a kernel of wheat falls to the ground and dies, it remains only a single seed. But if it dies, it produces many seeds" (John 12:24). It's an age-old principle that something must die before it can produce, before it can live. That's one reason the Christian

▼

does not need to fear death—we are simply transitioning, dying before we can live. I don't pretend to understand this principle. I just know it's true.

You are the only one who knows for sure whether or not your dream has died a complete death.

"I have finally touched my dream and now you're saying I'm supposed to let it die?" I can hear you saying. "What kind of crazy talk is that?"

I'm not saying the dream you're touching now should have to die. But if, as a child, you entertained the dream, lost it, and have now finally touched it again, the time in between was its death. You may have mourned the end of a dream, thinking it was gone forever, but the point is, the dream was supposed to die. It's part of the plan.

Look at what happened to the disciples' dream. They planned to make Jesus their king and set up His kingdom on earth. They served Him with this end in mind. Imagine their grief on the day of His death. What was happening to their dream?

They were lucky. They only had to watch their dream die for three days, long days to be sure, because they didn't know what to think or do. They ended up going fishing.

At the end of three days Jesus exploded on the scene once again, this time as their risen king. What's three days when at the end of it you get a king?

During the time our dream is dying, I believe God is adjusting, reorchestrating, and fine tuning our hearts to receive our dream again in its new form. The passions that drive our new dream will be God-driven instead of self-driven. It's an important time, a time that can't be short-circuited.

Jesus wasn't twiddling His thumbs during those three days between His death and resurrection. He had lots to do—ripping Satan's dominion wide open.

During the time our dream is dying, we should be doing soul work, preparing for that moment when we sense the first signs of life—our dream is about to live again. Soul work is growing, pondering, brainstorming, healing, grieving and preparing the soil in our soul for the time when we will sow the seed of our dream.

I wish I had understood this process as I walked through the dark night of my soul. An understanding of the process keeps us from becoming hopeless when we see nothing happening, when our dreams seem illusive and passion seems out of our grasp.

It's true that often a person's dream dies never to be resurrected. I know a few people I can honestly say are living their dreams. Maybe it's the day we live in. It takes so much energy just to survive in the nineties. Who has the energy to go chasing after illusive dreams? We find it easier to turn on the television and watch Barbara Walters interview someone else who's doing it. It's less threatening, too. We can vicariously enjoy the momentary thrill without putting in any of the necessary work.

I think part of the reason these dead dreams aren't resurrected is because many, if not most, people don't even know they can be. Not only can they be resurrected, but we can do anything we want with them once we bring them up. Most often, we do need to do something with them. They need some adjusting—some fine tuning.

Adjusting Your Dream(s)

As I've mentioned other places in this book, what's important is not so much what we do, but what's driving us to do it—the passion. What's the passion? Is it love? Is it fear? Is it anger?

Maybe as a child you wanted to be a pilot, or a disc jockey, or a spy. Why?

As children, we have a heightened sense of adventure, a belief in our invincibility, and a kind of wonder that tells us anything is possible. I'll just do this. I'll be this. Fun.

Then reality kicks in at some point. Someone, a teacher, a parent, or a sibling says something like, "Are you crazy? You can't do that." We experience our first doubt. Someone says something else, adding to our pile of self-doubt. Someone might even laugh at us. Doubt upon doubt builds, and finally we say, "They're right. I can't do that." We might even take it as far as, "I can't do anything."

It might be necessary for us to line up in our minds all of those people who told us we couldn't do stuff (*you fill in the blank with what you would do to them*) in order to get back on track. Do whatever it takes. Don't ever let another person steal your dream. No one in the world has the right to do that.

When we finally do recover our dream, it's never in quite the same shape as when we lost it. It looks different somehow, and it should. Anything looks different seen through the eyes of a fifty-five-year-old as compared to a ten-year-old. We're different people.

I remember going to Disneyland at ten and then again when I was about thirty-five. The Magic Kingdom didn't seem as big as I'd remembered.

So don't be confused or discouraged if your dream doesn't look or feel quite the same as it once did. It simply needs a little adjusting, or a little tweaking, or a little focusing.

I doubt if every president of the United States dreamed as a boy about being that. Growing up, he might have imagined himself speaking to large numbers of people, but he might have been in the Boy Scouts at the time, or sergeant at arms of his fifth grade. How could he have ever known who he would someday be?

I'm wagering that he kept adjusting, tweaking, and focusing his dream. He had to. How else could one become president? It doesn't just happen because someone happens to know someone who happens to know someone who happens to know someone who thinks you'd be a good candidate and tells you to send in your resumé.

We must be willing to take action. A friend of mine has a son who wants to act and/or direct in Hollywood. Last year he was working in a restaurant in Washington. What's he doing right now? Nannying for a Hollywood producer and father of

▼

five. He's getting closer to making his dream a reality. I guarantee that the more he hangs around Hollywood the more he'll find himself adjusting his dream.

My fifteen-year-old daughter wants to sing and/or act. I've given her both voice and acting lessons, but she took a slight detour this year. She got pregnant.

I refuse to let her forget her dream. We'll just refocus a little bit after the baby comes. It may take her a little longer; she may have to work a little harder. That's OK. The only kind of dream worth pursuing is the kind we have to truly earn, the kind driven by our passion to be all that God intends for us to be.

OK, so you're willing to adjust your dream and to take another look and refocus. How do you make your dream a reality?

Making Your Dream a Reality

I suppose some people thought I was really stupid when I quit my very secure day job and took a flying leap into Freelance Land a few years ago. With no other job in sight and only a few dollars in the bank, what in the world was I thinking?

It was the way I had to do it. It's the way I always do things. That's what works for me. Contrary to popular opinion, I'm no fool. I know that most normal folks are a little less impulsive than I am and go about things more methodically, especially something as important as making a living.

For me, it's always sink or swim, all or nothing, live or die. I need that intense sense of urgency to make things happen. Yes, I believe in praying, planning, and thinking things through, but when it's time to jump, I have to do it right then or I know I never will.

I think I kind of let God do most of the planning and worrying about things. So far, He has always let me know in plenty of time when a big change is on the horizon.

For you, bringing your dream to life may mean taking out a big loan (that would quite honestly scare me to death—I like to travel light), enrolling in college, or slowly phasing out a family business—something that takes time and planning.

I find it fascinating how God is able to communicate Himself and His plans to our individual personalities. I absolutely know, would stake my life on the fact, that He wants us to live passionately and abundantly. But exactly how we do that varies from person to person.

If you're truly in touch with your passion, it will drive you and keep driving you to take the necessary steps toward fulfillment of your dream. Don't worry excessively about whether or not the dream is God's will. Some people spend their whole lives struggling with this. I believe if we've committed our hearts to Jesus Christ and He's redeemed our souls, then our dreams are redeemed also. I heard author and psychologist Larry Crabb say once that we can't wait for totally pure motives. If we wait for pure motives, we'll never do anything for God. How many of your actions could you honestly say are prompted from absolutely 100 percent pure motives?

So, we've allowed God to reprogram us, we've pondered the dream, and we've let it die. Now it's back. It becomes reality when we do one thing—move. Dreams only come true for those who move. It starts with a single step.

We must always count the cost, but not to the point that it paralyzes us. We count the cost and consider the risks, then we move. Moving is the nod that God waits for. He's right there—as long as we're willing to move. Never will He do it all for us.

One friend of mine has just started training because next year she plans to climb Mount Rainier. If you've ever seen this mountain, you understand why she's in training.

Another friend, whose dream is to someday become an opera singer, has just been offered a job in Vienna. The move will take her closer to fulfilling this dream, so she's taking the job.

Yet another friend has dreamed for many years of opening a home for people with head injuries. He took classes, researched the project, completed all kinds of tests, and filled out hundreds

▼

of forms—each of these was a step toward his dream. Last year he finally received his license and rented a huge home. He has six residents now. He is living out his dream.

Fueled by passion we can make our dreams a reality and keep them a reality.

Keeping Your Dream Alive

Dreams are fragile. They're illusive and delicate. They drift away when we're not paying attention. They wilt when not nurtured. They die a real death when forgotten.

I wonder what would have happened if Jesus let Peter and Andrew distract Him with fishing one too many times. Where would we be? Impossible, you say, but He was human as well as divine, and in His humanness He must have had moments of distraction, moments where He had to plead with His Father to help Him stay focused. Of course, dying on a rugged cross isn't exactly our idea of a dream come true. Nonetheless, it was His plan, His purpose. It was what He came to earth to do. It was His passionate calling.

In the harsh light of reality our dream may not look at all like we thought it would. It may be an entirely different color and shape than we had envisioned, but as we pray and ponder, we often come to the realization that we are pursuing more than a dream—we are pursuing a calling.

When I became a wife and a mother, it wasn't the fulfilling of a long-held dream. I was not one of those young teenagers who dreamed of some day getting married, and having children and a home with a picket fence. When it happened and I was living it, it was like a serendipity. I welcomed it. I realized that being a mother was a calling, and it still is. When I became a writer, it was definitely a dream come true and a calling as well.

Dreams come to us in different ways. The "mother thing" is a hard one for me, especially as my children have become teenagers. I have created, watched die, and recreated more dreams than I can ever count. I feel like the dreams concerning what I want for me and my children have died a thousand deaths. God and I keep resurrecting them, and every once in a while I see the kind of forward movement that lets me know we're making progress. That's all I need—hope.

It's not sheer determination that keeps our dreams alive. It's not positive thinking or willpower. It's God-given passion that fuels our dreams as long as we stay on the passionate edge.

———

FOURTEEN

▼

MAKING YOUR WORLD GO 'ROUND

Love does indeed make the world go 'round, but I'd like to take that time-worn phrase a little further. *Passionate* love makes the world go 'round—God's kind of passionate love.

There's a huge difference between love as it's communicated by the media and romance novels and the sacrificial kind of love that Jesus exemplified on the cross and continues to exemplify in the true Christian's life. God's kind of love is driven by the passion that comes from knowing God on a personal level.

Love is a word that we may first hear spoken by a parent: "I love you." It feels warm, cozy, and, oh, so secure.

Love is a word that a person of the opposite sex whispers in the back seat of a car. It feels warm, cozy, and, oh, so secure. It may turn out to be devastating, selfish, and humiliating. That word, driven by sinful need, may momentarily ruin our lives.

Love is a word that men and women who abuse each other scream out. Cults talk about it and then commit mass suicide. Child molesters smile and use it to manipulate.

It's confusing sometimes. What is love? What is passionate love? How can God expect us to love, really love such a violent and hateful world?

Sometimes it seems like a joke that I'm supposed to love the jerk who cut in front of me on the freeway this morning, or the idiot who tore the pages that I needed out of the phone book in the phone booth, or the thief who burglarized all the cars in the parking lot at Wild Waves last week and ripped off my car stereo.

These are minor infractions. What about the neighbor who lured my child into his car, took her out in the middle of nowhere, and threatened to make her walk home if she didn't do what he said? Or the little girl who ran over my son's leg and snapped it in two, and whose family (they lived next door) refused to talk to us again because they didn't want to be slapped with any medical bills? Or the couple who bought my living room set and then skipped town without paying me?

The above are all true incidents, and these people were all neighbors. How do we live with these kinds of people, let alone passionately love them? It seems an impossible task.

As I cite all of the above negative situations, it sounds like my cynical side is coming out again. There are plenty of nice folks around who stay in their own lanes on the freeway and leave yellow pages intact in phone booths. The Bible says it's easy to love those who love us; it's loving our enemies that gets a little tricky.

By the way, I know for a fact that certain individuals have found it difficult to love me at times. I'm not saying I've never cut anyone off on the freeway or been someone's pain in the neck on any one day.

The reason we're focusing on loving the difficult people here is because: (1) it seems like there are so many of them, and (2) if we don't learn to aggressively, passionately, and redemptively love our world, we'll respond to it in other ways such as in hostility or self-protection.

Too often we quote the Scripture, "All men will know that you are my disciples, if you love one another" (John 13:35), hug our brother and sister in Christ, and then pat ourselves on the back for showing love to the world.

I'm not convinced God's impressed with that kind of love. I'm not sure the world is either. Although I will admit it is rather miraculous these days when two people, two families, two neighborhoods, or two countries can live next to each other with any degree of harmony.

I believe, in God, it is possible to love the world's representatives that, often unexpectedly, step into our path each day. I also believe it's some of the most difficult emotional labor we ever engage in, and we need to walk on the passionate edge to do it.

Before the passionate edge, when unlovable types (to me) came along, I repressed any hostile feelings I might have. My goal simply became to keep myself and my children safe and to do whatever else it might take to deal with them. I thought this was the best thing to do *when* I had a choice. Sometimes I didn't and gritted my teeth and waited for them to go away. It wasn't until I understood the power of things like empathy, tolerance, forgiveness, cultural sensitivity, and *passion* that my love for the world and the hard-to-love (for me) types became real, and godly.

Staying Culturally Sensitive

I attended a conference recently where I heard a preacher speak out against cultural sensitivity. "All of this cultural sensitivity stuff is garbage," he ranted. "The Word of God never changes. What God said two thousand years ago, four thousand years ago, still goes. David and Bathsheba's story is repeated down through the ages. Sin doesn't change and neither does God's way of dealing with it. And that's all you need to know."

These kinds of sermons tend to run together in my mind. They all sound the same.

▼

But, for the sake of example, if Jesus Christ were born to a virgin, say, in the sixties, we know He wouldn't show up thirty-three years later, today, in a robe and sandals. He might be wearing a business suit and driving a Lexus. More likely, He'd be in jeans and a workshirt. And His death might be the result of a drive-by shooting at the hands of gang members.

We've heard all of those arguments. How Jesus would show up is not so much the point as is the fact that He takes us where we are and that the day and age that we live in *does* matter. If I want to passionately love the world I live in today, I can't pretend that technology doesn't exist, that abortion is decreasing, and that violence isn't a reality. These things are all a reality, and that's not all. What about AIDS, child molestation, and crooked politicians? These things are all more prevalent than even ten years ago, and while I don't see everything about today's culture as totally negative, I can't ignore the reality of the difficulty of loving this kind of world.

As the managing editor of a parenting magazine, I'm on a balancing beam all of the time. I have to constantly balance where our readers are with where I believe many of our children really are. It's tough. Many parents are in denial about what their children are thinking, and they certainly don't want to hear us tell them.

Recently, we ran a story about a Christian kid, Jordan, who calls himself a "graffiti artist," and is addicted to drawing (or tagging) downtown buildings. We received letters asking why we ran this interview. Our readers wanted to know why we would want to glorify vandalism.

We ran the story to educate our readers and help them understand and accept kids in our culture today, kids like Jordan, so that when given the opportunity, our readers could relate to these kids from a place of grace rather than judgment and condemnation.

My goal to bridge this particular gap has everything to do with cultural sensitivity. "Graffiti artists," or vandals, or whatever you choose to call them are a part of our culture, like it or not. They're not going to go away, no matter how much we rant and rave about the damage, no matter how many times we keep painting over their "art." They'll keep coming back.

So what does God expect of us? To grow in passionate love just as He did for the misunderstood people of His time. They are not just "hoodlums" as we might like to think. God looks at them and sees people worth loving and dying for.

That's a tough assignment, to passionately love these kids who are forever "tagging" our city buildings. I have a theory about what it might take to reach them, and it can be summed up in one word—relationship. They won't damage the property of their *friends*.

Jesus was "a friend of tax collectors and 'sinners'" (Matt. 11:19). The tax collectors and sinners of today may be dressed a little differently as graffiti artists, computer programmers, and driven feminists—but building relationships works pretty much the same from generation to generation.

If we care at all about the culture we live in, we must commit ourselves to grow in passionate love for those in that culture.

Growing in Tolerance

To me, godly tolerance is not putting up with the other person; it's quiet acceptance of, learning to appreciate, the other person. God's kind of passion always goes beyond what we might expect or think we're capable of. We're always capable of more than we think we are.

A few years ago when I started a job at a Christian ministry, I noticed right away that my fellow employees approached their Christian experience in a vastly different way than I did. Their form of prayer and worship was not one I was comfortable with. I was skeptical of some of their methods in approaching God, and they weren't comfortable with the kinds of books I was reading and the music I liked.

It was tough going as we checked each other out—a lot of mistrust, challenging questions, and tense discussions. Over the years, because we were committed to working together and to the ministry's goals, we grew in respect for and understanding of one another. Today, even as I've moved on to another form of employment, some of them remain my best friends.

We learned tolerance, how to live and work next to each other and accept, even celebrate, our differences.

I believe life on the passionate edge is, for the most part, one of great joy, fulfillment, and satisfaction. However, we reap those benefits only after a lot of hard work. Growing in tolerance, while ultimately quite rewarding, is some of the hardest work we'll ever do on this journey because loving those who are different from us takes more understanding than we humanly have.

Growing in tolerance takes at least three things: (1) validation of the other person's approach, viewpoint, or life-style, (2) willingness to try to identify with the other person, understand a different viewpoint, or find a meeting place, and (3) commitment to accept and celebrate the other person whether or not we ever agree or understand that person's unique life experience.

Validation

We validate when we acknowledge the other person's experience and honor it by listening, hearing, and caring. Validation takes place when we simply want to know who the other person is. Hostile, nonproductive arguments occur when people aren't listening to one another, when they don't stop talking to hear each other.

Too often, when my teenagers are trying to relate their experiences to me, instead of listening I'm planning my next barrage. Their experiences are so different from mine, and sometimes they scare me. Maybe I don't think what they have to say is as important as what I have to say, but at these times we can go no further. Communication can't take place until validation does.

Willingness

Once we validate the other person, we have to go even further and find a place to identify with that person's unique experience. How can we relate to this experience, no matter how bizarre it may sound?

I have a hard time with abortion. As a woman's "choice," it bothers me terribly, but if I want to communicate with a person without judgment, maybe a friend who has had an abortion, I only have to reach for the feeling of discovering what it would be like, as a single woman, to suddenly discover that today at forty-three I'm pregnant. My children are almost grown. I'm finally getting myself together financially. . . . It doesn't take long for me to identify with my friend, even though I can't imagine myself doing such a thing. Whether or not I would ever act on the feeling is not the issue. I can understand. I can identify. I can understand not wanting to be pregnant. That's enough.

Commitment

Accepting is one thing; celebrating is quite another. As I mentioned earlier, if we don't commit to accept and celebrate others and their different experiences, we'll relate to our world from a place of fear which often acts itself out in hostility.

I'm not talking about accepting evil—it must be confronted. But we lose the opportunity to confront evil if we're unwilling to grow in tolerance of those who commit evil acts. Jesus was a tolerant man—He loved sinners passionately. His passionate love and tolerance for them is what earned Him the right to relate, develop friendships, and speak truth into their lives.

The Art of Empathy and Compassion

"Those who never learn to empathize are the most dangerous human beings on earth. They're ambulatory sociopaths, and they can be on Wall Street as well as in Attica prison."[1] Andrew Vachss spoke these words in an interview with Walter Anderson, editor of *Parade* magazine, several years ago. Vachss works as an attorney and legal guardian appointed by the state to represent children who are both victims and predators. If anyone would know what goes into the making of a psychopath, he would.

Empathy is the identifying with another's suffering, and compassion is the desire to alleviate that suffering.

I remember the days of feeling absolutely helpless and totally inept in the face of anyone's suffering. I just didn't know what to do. My most intense feeling at these times was not one of empathy or compassion but self-consciousness—a kind of get-me-out-of-here feeling.

This was before the passionate edge, during my numb days. Empathy and compassion are about learning to feel the pain of others. It takes just as much courage. The reason for learning passionate empathy and compassion for others is so we don't hurt them and we can relate to them with God's kind of love.

A friend of mine recently poured her heart out to her mother about her depression. She was in counseling, discovering the root of it, but was in mortal agony.

"Mom, I don't know what to do," she sobbed. "I can't eat. I can't sleep. It's affecting my relationship with Bill [her husband]."

This was a long distance call, and there was a moment of silence on the other end of the line.

"I know what you mean," her mother said, finally. "Your sister called me yesterday. She's having a hard time finding a house she likes."

What? Is this the twilight zone? Her mother, unable to empathize, likened her daughter's near suicidal depression to her other daughter's frustration because she couldn't find a house that suited her. This daughter needed her mother to hear her, to care, and to feel empathy and compassion.

Without passion, true empathy and compassion are impossible. Because empathy comes from our soul's ability to universally connect with others in our world, we must have touched our passionate self in order to be empathetic.

What happens inside of you when people pour out their hearts? Are you the one hurting people choose to talk to? How do you express your care when another person is hurting? Or do you?

Hurting people are all around us. Jesus longs to express His great love and care through us. We're all He has. He wants to infuse us with passion so that it might drive us to the kind of empathy and compassion that actually does something to alleviate the sufferings of others.

I have a friend who every so often, when she knows I'm overwhelmed with work or children, insists on coming over and cleaning my house. She vacuums, scrubs floors, and cleans toilets. That's empathy with my stress. That's compassion in action. That's the kind of passion that motivates one to do good.

On-the-Edge Forgiveness

I'm trying to convince myself that it's because I have five children and the odds are greater, but for whatever reason, we've had several run-ins with the police.

After a recent, especially humiliating experience with a law enforcement officer, the guilty child and I crossed a parking lot. Full of rage, I turned and gave my child a murderous look. "And after all I've done for you—guitar lessons, skiing lessons, horseback riding lessons, the time and money I've invested . . ."

I was prepared to withdraw every single thing and withhold any good thing until I had proof of change. I was about to give her even more pieces of my mind when suddenly I stopped.

God gives free gifts. He never makes us earn these gifts. He doesn't make us prove that we're good enough, perfect enough to have them—He just gives. No strings attached.

And I realized that once again, just as I felt passionate fury at this situation, I would have to offer passionate forgiveness so that I could keep giving, respecting, and someday trusting and loving.

"So are you taking away my guitar lessons this week?" my child asked later as we talked about it.

"No," I said.

I would find another way to vent my fury and discipline my child—a way that had nothing to do with what my child deserved to receive or what I had to give, a way that reinforced respect and honor in my child and still enabled me to forgive the crime.

Passionate forgiveness "guts" through the pain of betrayal, fights and conquers the tendency to self-protect, and reaches out in love again, all the while holding the other person accountable.

We begin to understand the concept of forgiveness when we begin to understand God's role in our lives. I don't believe in the power of forgiveness outside of Him; I don't believe it's possible. Forgiveness remains pretty much just that—a concept—until the passionate edge.

Passionate forgiveness is not an option but a life commitment. It's part of the package when we think about relating to our world on the passionate edge.

In one way, passionate forgiveness as a commitment is more difficult because as humans we're experts at finding the easy way out, getting ourselves off the hook, looking for the exit route. Passionate forgiveness blocks all the exits.

In another way, passionate forgiveness is less difficult because when forgiveness is fueled by godly passion we are more motivated to do the loving thing—for God and others, as well as ourselves. This kind of forgiveness commits to "gut" through the issue(s) as long as it takes for healing.

I'm still forgiving my mother and still asking for forgiveness from her, and she's been dead four years. It's just that we didn't resolve everything while she was alive. Since I'm committed to the passion-filled life, stuff comes up once in a while that still connects the two of us and off I go once again, "gutting" through whatever the painful issue is so that I can forgive and be forgiven—ultimately, so that I may love God and my world with absolute and total abandonment.

Loving with Abandonment

To abandon means to yield completely. It's an unrestrained freedom of actions or emotions. It's to say yes all the way, no matter what. It's to act without inhibitions, caution, or even thought. It shoots not from the hip but the heart. It's to throw, thrust, and fling yourself toward the target. It's to not worry, panic, or fret about the results of your throwing, thrusting, and flinging. It's to dance freely and spontaneously along the passionate edge without concern over what you're wearing, who's watching, and where you're headed. It's the way God wants us to love.

———

FIFTEEN

▼

THE PASSION-FILLED LIFE

I awoke from a dream once, my pillow soaked with tears. I dreamed in living color and with intense emotion that my second son, Dwight, had died. He was about five years old at the time. I don't remember how he died in the dream, only that I felt the most incredible sadness and the most incredible relief to find it was only a dream. What could compare to losing a child? I can't think of anything. Yet, losing our passion is one of the greatest losses we can experience because it means we aren't able to feel love for not only a child but anyone who happens to be in our lives. We're not able to receive love either. Losing our passion has to be one of the greatest losses of our entire lives.

It doesn't have to happen, and once we've discovered the passionate edge, it's probably less likely to happen because we are so acutely aware of our feelings that we immediately know when we're beginning to slip.

However, we can never let down our guard, not for a moment. We can never assume that we're beyond losing that precious edge of passion because now it has become a lifestyle for us.

Since passion affects every area of our lives, it sometimes happens that we can be slipping in one area even while soaring in others. Allowing ourselves to slip at all could indicate an overall problem; we might be too content, losing our sharp edge, or we might be experiencing fear, causing us to pull back from experiences that mean risk or danger. If we allow ourselves to slip too far or let it go on for too long, we might very well end up dull once again, the passionate edge only a memory.

Recently I watched the movie *The River Wild*. The main character, played by Meryl Streep, faces more life-threatening dangers and losses in this two-hour movie than most of us will face in a lifetime. The movie's setting is a dangerous river-rafting trip where she risks her life to save her family. When Streep was interviewed about what motivated her to take this particular script, she answered, "I wanted my kids to see that Mommy was still cool."

As I watched the movie, I couldn't help but admire Streep. Instead of relying on stuntwomen, she did all of the scary rafting scenes herself. I thought, *I do all this talking about passion, and I'm still observing life in too many ways instead of participating in it.* It was embarrassing. I wanted to look around the movie theater to see if anyone had read my thoughts.

I watch a lot of movies, the more suspenseful and full of emotion, the better. I read novels but only those with characters who live passionately. I cultivate friendships with people who are risk-takers and daredevils. This way I can vicariously experience everyone else's "daring adventures" while I stay safe and cozy at home.

I was disgusted with myself. This is a recent revelation, by the way, so I'm still in the throes of trying to figure out exactly what to do about it.

I'm talking plain and simple here about physical, daring adventures. I do pretty well in other areas. Anyway, something is on the horizon for me. I can feel it, and I'm ready. I think.

The point is now that I've seen the problem, I don't dare let myself slip any further. It would be a great loss to get to the end of my life (and that could be at any moment, of course) and look back knowing that fear held me in its grip, that I let many opportunities on the passionate edge slide by because I was too paralyzed with fear to grab them. After all, I've believed in and taught others about the passionate edge. I would feel like an impostor.

I'm on the passionate edge. I plan to stay on the passionate edge. Is there a way to make sure that happens? What can we do when we feel ourselves start to slide? Or, if you're like me, what if you wake up some day and realize you're not really dancing along the passionate edge in every area like you thought you were?

Maintaining a Fresh Perspective

In other places in this book, we've talked about questioning, but it bears repeating here—question, question, question, not necessarily out loud, but at least to yourself or to a good friend. Especially question those things everyone seems to accept so easily. Check everything out. Everything. Don't take anybody's word for anything.

Hang out with people, all kinds of people. Don't write anyone off because they're too conservative, too weird, too rich (especially not too rich!), too old, or too young. Cultivate friendships with lots of different kinds of folks.

Watch talk shows. Don't be afraid of conflict. Debate ideas with people you know hold a different view than you do. If it gets heated, don't worry about it, especially if (1) the person is your spouse or an old friend and has loved and accepted you through worse, or (2) you'll never see the person again. The important thing is that you keep getting new insights, growing, and looking at life in a fresh way.

I love it when someone says something and I think, "Oh wow, I never thought about it like that before." This seldom happens because most of us tend to talk to the same old people about the same old stuff every day.

"What if . . . . " Those words, uttered in all sincerity, may be two of the most important words you can say. "What if" suggests unlimited possibilities for discovery. "I wonder" works just as well. Said in the right context with the right person, these words will take you to new places.

Get out of your house. This may seem obvious, but we sit around the house and then wonder why we don't have a life.

For example, my daughter is currently a live-in nanny. She found herself becoming more and more depressed and wondering why. It only took a couple of trips with the children down to the park a block from where she lives to meet some people her own age. Almost overnight she began to develop a full life with all kinds of friends, simply because she left her house.

Cobwebs collect in our minds so easily. The daily routine will do it. If we do the same things day in and day out, before we know it we are less than stimulating to be around. We're old before we're old, if you know what I mean. This is really all about staying awake—change, vibrancy, spontaneity, aliveness.

Surprise yourself. You won't lose your passion if you can keep surprising yourself. Pretend you don't know yourself and do something totally wild, unpredictable, and different than you might do if you knew yourself.

I think today may be one of the most difficult times to live in as far as trying to maintain a passionate life. Everything around us compels us toward security, safety, and a contented life far from the edge. In such a world how do we hold onto our position on the edge?

Guarding Your Passion

To guard something indicates a possessive watching over, protecting, and keeping safe. This is what we must do if we want to hold onto our passion.

However, in this case the way to guard it is not to lock it in a box for safekeeping as we would a material treasure. No, in this case, the way to guard it is to make sure we're always expressing it.

I recently attended the book reading of a person who I have greatly admired over the years as one who has a tremendous amount of courage in her one-woman battle against an unjust system in our country. I could hardly control myself as I sat in my chair listening intently to this woman speak humbly and passionately about her cause.

As I stood in line later waiting for her to autograph my book, I couldn't believe I was actually getting to meet this person.

It was my turn. She took my book, autographed it, and then looked me right in the eye. "You send wonderful non-verbals," she said.

She had received my passionate response to her presentation. This is my desire in living on the passionate edge—that others would receive life. Now I know that others will not always be able to sense it in the way this woman did; I believe she was also very much in touch with her passionate side. But I hope they will intuitively sense the vibrancy and wonder that says, "This is a great day to be alive and to live for God, and I'm so pleased we're sharing this moment."

It's not that difficult to communicate once you get the hang of it. It's an attitude we wake up with in the morning and take to the breakfast table and into every conversation we have with every person throughout the day. We take it to bed at night and even into our dreams. My dreams these days, since I've embraced the passionate edge, are filled with risky situations, intense emotions, and impossible feats, all played out in living color with me in the center doing battle with the elements, the dark figures that represent evil, and often enjoying the sweet taste of victory when passion is reigning in my conscious life.

Whenever I leave my house, I'm conscious that I may face various situations that may call for all kinds of passionate responses on my part, and I pray that God will show Himself strong. A *daring adventure* is indeed the perfect phrase for how I want to live.

To guard your passion is to stay conscious and awake, something I've referred to often in this book. If you can stay conscious and awake, you'll never have to worry about losing your passion for longer than a moment. The devil can't steal it from you because you've never taken your eyes off of it. He certainly can't destroy it because God has put His seal on it. If our hearts are turned toward the Lord in everything we do and all that we are, our passion will stay intact. Finally, there is no way the devil can kill our passion because it is our soul and our soul belongs to God, just as do our hearts. I suppose ultimately what I'm saying is that what we must protect more than anything else is our relationship with our Lord—nurture it, keep it alive, and stir it up. We do this moment by moment.

Living in the Moment

Sometimes funny things stick in my mind. Who knows why I will always remember the day my nine-year-old son came home from a friend's house muttering and complaining.

"I don't see why we can't get a barbecue," he whined. "They have a barbecue. It's cool. You cook stuff outside. How come we don't have a barbecue?"

I was glad my friend didn't have a yacht because acquiring a barbecue was in the realm of possibility. This particular son had a habit of complaining about good times because he couldn't tangibly possess them, and so he would become depressed.

"Can't you just enjoy the cookout?" I asked him.

"No," he said.

This son needed to learn to live in and enjoy the moment. Over the years, I've realized, though, as much as I hate to admit this, I often do the same thing. I may be with someone I really admire, have a great time, and then come home and do nothing

▼

but berate myself because I lack the qualities in that person that I so admire. I forget the moment and how precious it was.

I want to learn to go to the cookout, live in the smells, sounds, and tastes of the moment, and come home thankful for the experience.

Living on the edge means learning about ourselves, and yes, we must always be open to whatever each experience has to teach us. It's perfectly normal to want and desire those things that we lack, especially when we have the opportunity to experience them, even vicariously. We are not meant to possess everything that we experience. Sometimes the memory is all we can possess. Maybe that's why so many of us fear living in the moment. We can't even possess our moments. They are fleeting. They pass quickly, never to be experienced again in any form. If we can learn to live them passionately, they will become a part of us, and I suppose, in some way, we do possess them.

To live in the moment is to live with the knowledge that we are indeed eternal beings and that we can make a particular moment matter for all eternity. It is to live with a huge sense of significance, not arrogance but significance. We know we matter and each moment is full of tremendous meaning because of that.

We are not accidents. God has ordained for us to live on the earth at this time, and what we do and who we are does make a difference. Feel heavy? It is, but it's not like we have to go around thinking how significant we are all the time, bearing the weight of making every moment intensely purposeful. We settle the purposefulness in our hearts and minds and then we simply live with the humble knowledge that God will bring about the passionate purpose for us in each moment. All we have to do is stay tuned in, but it's truly amazing how difficult that is with all of the earthly distractions that come at us every day. It's a lifelong practice, learning to live in the moment, but I figure if I even learn a small fraction about how to do it, I'll be ahead of where I was last year or even a moment ago.

Living in the moment means keeping your wits about you at all times so that nothing slides by you and so that you can walk in integrity.

Walking in Passionate Integrity

We can only live the true passion-filled life if we are people of integrity. The passion lovers I know are also people of integrity. They are expressers of their passion(s) for a reason and purpose that is higher than what it may look like on the surface.

I am criticized for admiring certain people. But I don't admire people so much for what they do or what they represent as much as I do for their courage in standing up for what they believe and their walk in integrity in the face of great opposition. Let me clarify this: I never admire people who represent evil.

As on-the-edge lovers of passion, we must be willing to stand up for what we passionately believe God to be saying on any one issue, shouting it from the housetops, if necessary. Passion is not something we can repress or should repress when God is calling us to integrity.

We fall short of God's plan when we are only concerned about maintaining the passionate life once we've grasped it. We must also courageously live it out in front of God and everyone, both friends and enemies. I'm glad God has more than an abundant amount of grace because this happens step by step. It's simply a stance of willingness to express ourselves when God says we must.

Living out the passionate life can be a constant struggle because anytime we let someone know who we are, we face the possibility of rejection. While this may not be so hard with the folks we run into every day on the street, it becomes very difficult when we try to do this with our family and close friends. We are called to integrity every day.

Let's say your friend is considering abortion—do you tell her about yours so long ago? You have just been hired at a new job and at lunch on the first day, the other employees start blasting Christians—do you tell them who you are? If not today, when? You're at a movie with friends and suddenly the plot is one that troubles your value system and the longer you sit there the more graphic it becomes. It's a comedy and everyone else is laughing. Does walking in integrity mean you make a statement by getting up and walking out? Do you make your statement over coffee after the movie? Does the situation require that you stay silent for now? Most importantly, can you do whatever it is the moment is requiring of you?

As you can see, the opportunities that call for integrity are endless. We may not always do the best thing for the moment. That's not as important as our awareness of the moment so that when it comes, we're alert, and it is unable to pass us by without our giving conscious thought to the most honest action for us at that time.

If this all seems like a lot of work, sometimes it is. Most of the time it's a very simple journey of living passionately ever after because it's a journey that we have chosen.

Living Passionately Ever After

To live happily or passionately or miserably ever after suggests that we will never waver from this state of being. As we think about the passionate edge, how we wish it were so, to have that kind of guarantee.

The truth is we can have that kind of guarantee. It is entirely up to us. The circumstances don't matter. The situation doesn't matter. Our feelings don't matter. All that matters is that we have made a decision to live passionately ever after. Therefore, when the storms come and shake the circumstances, the situation, and our feelings, we will rise to the storm. We will allow our passionate selves to take over and fight the battle with courage and integrity, in the face of pain and fear, and on the edge and in the presence of Almighty God.

I recently received a letter from a woman whose boyfriend died after an accident only weeks before he was to propose to her on a cruise in the Caribbean.

This illustrates the fact that you can't imagine what this next year has for you or how you'll grow from the experiences it gives you. If you will receive each experience as a gift, you will indeed grow. The passionate life does not come with a guarantee for happiness, but it does come with a guarantee for growth. So I hope growing is something you're interested in because that's what life on the passionate edge is all about.

"Life is either a daring adventure or nothing." May every moment of every day of your adventure be full of passion.

———

▼

NOTES

Introduction

1. Rosalie Maggio, *The Beacon Book of Quotations by Women* (Boston: Beacon Press, 1992), 188.

Chapter One

1. Rosalie Maggio, *The Beacon Book of Quotations by Women* (Boston: Beacon Press, 1992), 300.

2. Irving Stone, *The Agony and the Ecstasy* (New York: Doubleday & Co., 1961), 754.

Chapter Three

1. John Bradshaw, *Homecoming* (New York: Bantam Books, 1990), 233.

Chapter Four

1. Rosalie Maggio, *The Beacon Book of Quotations by Women* (Boston: Beacon Press, 1992), 25.

2. Larry Crabb, *Inside Out* (Colorado Springs, Colo.: NavPress, 1991), 87.

Chapter Five

1. Scott Peck, *The Road Less Traveled: A New Psychology of Love, Traditional Values, and Spiritual Growth* (New York: Touchstone Books, 1980).

▼

Chapter Seven
1. Edwin W. Teale, *The Thoughts of Thoreau* (New York: Dodd, Mead & Company, 1962), 235.

Chapter Twelve
1. Kathryn Arnold, "The Creative Spirit" *Delicious!* (September 1993), 14.
2. Marshall Cook, *Freeing Your Creativity* (Cincinnati, Ohio: Writer's Digest Books, 1992), 35.

Chapter Thirteen
1. Rosalie Maggio, *The Beacon Book of Quotations by Women* (Boston: Beacon Press, 1992), 89.

Chapter Fourteen
1. Walter Anderson, *The Greatest Risk of All* (Boston: Houghton Mifflin Company, 1988), 207.